ISBN: (13) 979-8-9875453-2-4 (Paperback)

Printed by Ernestine Robinson Hurtt Self Published, in the United States of America.

First printing, 2023.

Ernestine Robinson Hurtt – Self-Publisher
Freedom From Soul Pain – Seeing the
presence of God through pain
PO Box 426
Owings Mills, Maryland 21117

www.E RHurttAuthor.com
www.WomenSeekingTheKingdomcom.

The Pain Only God Can Heal

A Calming Psalm That Nourishes the Soul

Psalms 23

The Lord is my shepherd; I shall not want.
He makes me to lie down in green pastures;
He leads me beside the still waters.
He restores my soul; He leads me in the paths of righteousness
For His name's sake.
Yea, though I walk through the valley of the shadow of death,
I will fear no evil; For You are with me; Your rod and Your staff,
they comfort me.
You prepare a table before me in the presence of my enemies;
You anoint my head with oil;
My cup runs over.
Surely goodness and mercy shall follow me All the days of my life;
And I will dwell in the house of the Lord
Forever.

New King James Version

Table of Contents

A Calming Psalm That Nourishes the Soul

Part One

God Will Never Leave You Nor Forsake You

Part Two

The Transforming Power of God's Grace

Part Three
Everyone Needs the Lord and Savior Jesus Christ

The Most High Dwelling Place

Dedication

I dedicate this book to God for giving me the wisdom to recognize He is my Heavenly Father and that He daily fills my life with His presence.

I dedicate this book to my grandmother, her loving and quiet spirit led me to accept and love Jesus Christ as my Lord and Savior as a child.

I dedicate this book to my husband whose heart is continually being transformed by the power of Almighty God.

I dedicate this book to my children who are my precious gifts from God.

I dedicate this book to my classmate Dedra Swimpson for encouraging me to write this book. She saw something in me that

I could not see.

Introduction

*According to BrainsPotential.com research shows that,
"Psychological trauma occurs as the result of an extraordinary
stressful event that diminishes or destroys your sense of security and involves a threat to life or safety. Traumatic experiences
exceed your ability to cope, and your ability to integrate emotions involved with the experience. Psychological trauma can
cause you to feel helpless and leave you struggling with upsetting
emotions, memories, and anxiety. It can also leave you feeling
numb, disconnected, and unable to trust others. When bad things
happen, it can take time to get over the pain and feel safe again.
Whether the trauma happened years ago or yesterday, you CAN
make healing changes and move forward with your life"* (https://
brainspotential.com/healthfromtrauma). The previous statement
is a professional medical diagnosis of trauma and pain. Internal,
and external forces are not the only forces that cause emotional traumas. *Soul pain* (spiritual pain) is the other force that can
cause pain. *Soul pain* is a type of pain that is widely ignored in
the world because its source is embedded in the spiritual heart of
man.

Soul pain caused by life's events can have a negative impact
on an individual. Also, man's sin nature can be the catalyst of
soul pain which ignites abuse of others and ungodly acts against
Almighty God. Sin causes all types of evil desires and wretchedness within the soul while creating an insatiable appetite for more
sin. The Bible says, "The one who does what is sinful is of the
devil, because the devil has been sinning from the beginning. The
reason the Son of God appeared was to destroy the devil's work"
(1 John 3:8 NIV). Deliberate sinning obstructs our precious
relationship with Almighty God. *Soul pain* capable of oppressing

an innocent victim is an incorporeal phenomenon that originates from Satan's assault on the soul. *Soul pain* causes heartache and agony in the soul and confusion or denial in the mind. There are many circumstances in life, both internal and external, that can effectuate *soul pain*. Regardless of the source, circumstances of *soul pain* cannot be resolved easily and are life-altering.

Soul pain is not cured through medication, traditional medical instrumentality, psychologic therapeutic approaches, holistic therapies, or psychic hotlines. No one is immune from *soul pain*. It does not discriminate based on race, age, gender, religion, ethnicity, or status in life. *Soul pain* strikes in many ways with many different outcomes. Sadly, many believers will suffer from *soul pain* without the direction and support needed to overcome the debilitating physical, mental, spiritual, and unexplained incidents in life resulting from *soul pain*. Manifestations arise such as: self-injury (identity crisis, suicide, low-self-esteem, self-contempt); injury by others (betrayal, physical and mental abuse, cyberbullying, abandonment, divorce, humiliation); incidents beyond the sufferer's control (illness, death of a love one, and a plethora of other known and unknown conditions); a sufferer's injury toward others (projection of unprovoked anger toward a loved one) and loneliness. These hurtful conditions will leave the sufferer with emotional challenges if not addressed. Medical doctors professionally address and cure mental and physical pain. However, only Jesus Christ can heal and cure spiritual *soul pain*. Without His divine intervention, the sufferer may hopelessly become trapped in his or her pain as *soul pain* creates life-long strongholds.

This book is not being declared as a cure for all pain caused by mental, emotional, or physical illnesses. Nor does this book diminish the superb work performed by healthcare professionals to assist people in pain. In fact, if an individual suffers *soul pain*, I strongly encourage him or her to seek any and all needed help. Additionally, I recommend he or she consider the vast benefits of suffering God's way. To suffer God's way is explained later in the book. Additionally, the book will examine both the many challenges caused by *soul pain* as well as the wonderful transformation Almighty God brings. Consequently, this book probes my personal experience with *soul pain*: what caused it, the effects, and steps I took in the removal of *soul pain*.

The book is trifurcated, the first section focuses on my personal experience with *soul pain* early in life and its elimination by the power of Jesus Christ. The second section of the book focuses on my life from late adolescence to the present. The third and final section of this book focuses on the believing sufferer's broken spirit caused by *soul pain,* how *soul pain* can be eliminated, and how believers can be made whole by Almighty God. Further, the spiritually broken sufferer or willful rebellious sufferer who insists on going his or her own way is shown both the necessity of turning from sin and the importance of turning to Almighty God. Lovingly, the sufferer's soul, heart, and mind can be changed by God's agape love.

It is my prayer that by sharing my personal journey through *soul pain*, the remedy I employed to eliminate it, and my ability to see the presence of Almighty God through my pain, you will be encouraged and inspired to pursue purpose past your pain. Despite the many negative events in my life, God's divine healing made me spiritually whole. My faith and trust in Jesus Christ are based on the demonstration of His power through every nefarious experience. Accordingly, every chapter of the book evidences the lively and active character of God's Word in the lives of His children; Jesus Christ as the Savior who saves sinners; and God the Holy Spirit as the believer's helper to live righteously. This book depicts God's Word as the fountain of spiritual knowledge and wisdom as well as the spiritual weapon against the consequences of *soul pain* and spiritual warfare. If God's Word is applied daily, life will become viable and complete.

The complete relief of *soul pain* begins and ends by the power of Almighty God. As a result, the Godhead is present throughout all facets of my life and in every story rehearsed in these pages. The stories also expose the sinful nature of fallen mankind, the effects of spiritual warfare, and the divine grace to overcome. Each chapter illustrates the devastating impact *soul pain* has on the spiritual, physical, mental, and emotional areas of a sufferer's life as well as the deliverance that comes with the Almighty God's intervention. Finally, this book is also a love story - showing: 1) brokenness in all humanity; 2) the need for a Savior, Jesus Christ; 3) God's love toward His children; 4) the methods in which He redeems His children back to Himself; 5) His children's love towards their Heavenly Father; and 6) His children's love toward one another.

This book is intended to highlight *soul pain* experienced by sufferers and the misguided use of world's remedies to relieve *soul pain*. The words Christian, believer, sufferer, and believing sufferer are interchangeable synonyms throughout the book. Names of individuals have been changed for privacy. Each beginning chapter scripture is methodically explained in the workbook to demonstrate how God's Holy Word effects lives. The companion workbook prompts the readers to become cognizant of their current spiritual state of faith; desire to delve deeper into their spiritual lives; gain wisdom to see life from a spiritual perspective; and draw closer in their relationship with Jesus Christ. While reading this book, meditate on God's Word to examine if *soul pain* is affecting your life and allow God to eradicate *soul pain* His way.

Prologue

In her youth and while she was developing an intimate relationship with Jesus Christ, *soul pain* frequently visited the author. Although her soul was broken, Jesus Christ was her anchor. The Bible says, "He heals the brokenhearted and binds up their wounds" (Psalm 147:3). By surrendering her life to Jesus Christ as her Lord and Savior, the author's heart was changed forever. Over time, God the Holy Spirit convicted her of her own sinfulness, healed her heart, calmed her mind; and soothed her soul. The gift of God the Holy Spirit quietly spoke to her in her youth and still speaks to her today. God the Holy Spirit descended deep into crevices of the author's soul to seek out *soul pain* that caused her so much pain. These crevices cannot be seen by the human eye nor can they be identified by medical devices. Eradication of *soul pain* occurs by the following: seeking and applying God's Holy Word in every circumstance in life; acceding to Jesus Christ; and yielding to the power of God the Holy Spirit. God the Holy Spirit equipped the author in ways to glorify Almighty God even at the lowest point in her life, deep in the valley of despair.

With the passage of time, the Godhead made the author's life whole physically, spiritually, mentally, and emotionally despite the trials and tribulations she endured. As a young child and a new believer in Jesus Christ, the author did not understand the many spiritual encounters that would occur early in her life nor the spiritual encounters that would come later in her life. She did not understand just how extremely close Almighty God was with her in dark times of *soul pain*. She did not know how intimately God knew her. The Bible says, "You know my sitting down and my rising up; You understand my thought afar off. You comprehend my path and my lying down, And are acquainted with all my ways. For there is not a word on my tongue, But behold, O Lord, You know it altogether." (Psalm 139:2-4). God knows everything about the author's life and ultimately, God's gifts of forgiveness, grace, and mercy administered by God the Holy Spirit eradicated *soul pain* within the author permanently.

Instinctively people try to avoid pain at any cost. In a diligent search to gain comfort from *soul pain*, a sufferer may turn to the world's abundant supply of counterfeit and sinful pain-relieving agents such as: abuse of alcohol, abuse of legal and illegal drugs, gluttony, sexual hedonism, pornography, and many other counterfeit options to relieve or eliminate the inconceivable pain deep within the soul. These counterfeit agents do not eliminate *soul pain,* they cause deeper pain. Many people wonder why they hurt so deeply, are depressed, confused, or why their lives are in such a disarray. Without them knowing, the sufferer may be experiencing *soul pain*. *Soul pain* can interfere with a sufferer's ability to function normally or to have a fruitful life. Thankfully the sufferer can freely go boldly to the throne of grace to be healed. The Bible says, "Let us then approach God's throne of grace with confidence, so that we may receive mercy and find grace to help us in our time of need" (Hebrews 4:16). The Godhead is crucial in thoroughly curing *soul pain,* sinful behaviors, while dispensing divine love and grace.

Several divine mysteries in the author's life are documented in this book. Her personal journey is written retrospectively describing her naïve youth, willful adolescence, young adulthood;

and her spiritual growth into a person fully surrendered to Jesus Christ. For years, the author was on an emotional roller coaster ride without being able to get off. Her spiritual life was out of control for a time, but God patiently waited for her to surrender her life to His Son, Jesus Christ and become His child.

Part One

God Will Never Leave You

Nor Forsake You

Chapter 1

The Silent Sufferer

"Though my father and mother forsake me,
the LORD will receive me".

(Psalm 27:10)

ॐॐॐॐॐॐ

My formative childhood years were the late 1950s and early 1960s. Life was quite different than it is today. People weren't so volatile and angry. Back then, most households consisted of both a father and mother and children obeyed their parents without hesitation. Children were able to play safely outside without parental supervision. Parents were not overly concerned about the moment harm could come to their children because neighbors watched over neighborhood children. They watched to both protect them and discipline them. Doing something wrong was an embarrassment, not just to the parents, but to the entire family. For bringing such shame on the family, the child would be disciplined twice for their wrongdoing: once by the neighbor and then by their parents.

Part of me wondered if it was because the Blue Law prevented businesses from opening on Sundays giving people a true day of rest. In fact, we didn't even shop at the mall after church. Jesus Christ was respected by business owners and so fervently worshipped in the home that most of the stores were not even open. Instead, Sundays were set aside for religious observance and spending time with the family. Prayer and the pledge of allegiance were recited every morning in school before class began. It was as if people knew prayer was a heavenly salve for the weary soul and communication with Almighty God. As a result, praying to God was the first choice to solve obstacles in life . . . not the last choice. There was broad acceptance to love and worship the God of heaven.

My immediate family was small and included my father, my mother, and myself. My many cousins substituted for the brothers or sisters I never had. Unfortunately, my parents were a dysfunctional couple who created an unstable home setting. They were not the kind of people I would deem "good role models." My parents had secrets that I never uttered until much later in life. In 1960, I remember my family lived a short time in a public housing development called Flag House Court. Public Housing wasn't the dangerous blight on the community it is considered today. I remember playing in the grassy area outside and running along the long clean hallways with my little friends. The neighborhood wasn't perfect, but I felt safe there.

I was fortunate not to be a latchkey kid because my mother did not work outside the home and was always there when I returned from school. My mother was born in Durham, North Carolina and had eight siblings. She and five of her siblings eventually moved to Baltimore, MD. As I grew up, they all passed away and she was the last surviving sibling in Maryland (I never knew her other three siblings). After coming from such a large family, you would think my mother and I would be close. We were not.

We never did those cute mother-daughter activities. She was my mother, and I was her responsibility. That's where it began and ended.

My father was born in Baltimore, Maryland and had two step-brothers, and one stepsister. My father was the youngest and only biological child of my grandparents. I was not close to my father, but I obeyed him because he was my father, and it was the right thing to do. My parents were not affectionate people. I don't remember my mother or father ever hugging me or telling me that they loved me. But I didn't miss out on those things. I had secret weapons: grandparents.

My father's parents lived on a small alley street in Baltimore City. They lived in a petite two-story end-of-row rowhome. If you looked out of my grandparent's dining room window, you could see rear yards of neighboring homes. Dogs ran along the fences and barked as people walked by. In the winter months, my grandfather kept the entire house warm with a black potbelly wood stove located in the dining room. When the stove got hot, it radiated a warm glow throughout the room. In the summer, Saturday mornings were routinely the days neighbors swept their front sidewalks, cleaned gutters of trash, and cleaned trash that collected in the backyards of their homes. With pride, neighbors meticulously cleaned their marble steps. Baltimore City was known for those gleaming white marble steps. The Afro Newspaper held a yearly Clean Block Campaign Competition and invited community leaders and residents to participate to win monetary prizes for keeping neighborhoods free of trash and garbage. The block leaders on my grandmother's street would join the competition yearly. I don't know if our block ever won an award, but it was fun seeing everyone outside on Saturdays.

The block on which my grandparents lived was a beautiful picture of who they were. My grandfather was a very nice man from Tennessee. I don't recall him ever working. He was always home when we visited. He would always give me big hugs when I came around. Those hugs more than compensated for the ones I wasn't receiving at home. My grandfather died on January 28, 1986. He loved me, but it was my sweet grandmother who had the most meaningful impact on my life. She was a domestic worker who worked until she was in her early 80s. At that point she was mostly a companion who swapped stories of times past with her employer.

I fully understand why her employer desired her company. She was a righteous woman of faith with a quiet and gentle spirit. I never heard her raise her voice, swear, or say a negative word about anyone. In fact, my earliest memory of God comes from the time I spent watching and learning from her. I still have visions of my grandmother reading her Bible. There was always an open Bible on my grandparents' kitchen table. It is because of my grandmother's influence that I submitted my life to Jesus Christ at an early age. She told me about Jesus Christ and that He would always love me. Believing her was easy because I always felt loved when I was with her. Even when her father, my great-grandfather, would visit from Virginia would be so loving and kind to me. You notice these things when they are missing from your home. That love and kindness may have been missing from my home but, because of my grandparents, it was never missing from my life. That beautiful soul found her rest February 13, 2000.

As a very young child, I vividly remember one warm spring evening during the Easter holiday, my mother and I visited my mother's sister. My aunt and young cousins were sitting in the living room watching the movie, *The Greatest Story Ever Told* on a black and white floor model TV. There was a scene in the movie that impacted my life forever. The scene was when Jesus Christ was nailed to the cross by his executioners. That scene overwhelmed me so dramatically it struck a chord in my soul. The image of Jesus Christ's hand being nailed to the wooden cross disturbed my spirit tremendously. I began to quietly cry and with every bang of the hammer, the harder and louder I cried. I saw Jesus Christ – the one my grandmother said would always love me – being placed between two men also on wooden crosses. Jesus Christ asked His father to forgive His executioners. "Father forgive them" Jesus said, "For they do not know what they are doing" (Luke 23:34). What love?

At that point, I was crying uncontrollably. My cousins were snickering at me because I was crying. My mother grabbed me and took me into the rear kitchen. She began shaking me and yelling at me to stop crying. I replied, "But Mom you don't understand. They are killing Jesus." My heart ached for Jesus Christ that evening. I was so heartbroken to see Him being nailed to the cross. I couldn't finish watching the movie. I didn't understand why the rest of my family did not feel the way I did. Jesus Christ was being nailed to the cross and he did nothing wrong. I felt confused, angry, hurt, and distraught. I wondered why people could be so cruel.

From that day on, Jesus Christ was real to me. The vision of the executioners nailing Jesus Christ to the cross was permanently etched into my memory. Thinking back, I wondered if I was too young to have watched that part of the movie. Or maybe my grandmother's influence, which had already resulted in me accepting Jesus Christ as my savior, was the linchpin for my emotional response. Afterall, I was watching someone who I loved and who loved me succumb to the vile experience of crucifixion. Only God knows the answer. What I did know for sure was that what I saw was horrific.

When I was nine years old, my father lost his job and our family moved in with his parents. We lived with my grandparents for one year. The memories of living with my grandparents were the happiest times of my childhood. Grandparents' love is a special type of love. The love I felt from my grandparents will never be forgotten. While living there, on summer afternoons, girls and boys rode their bikes, roller skated, and played hopscotch in the street where we lived. Neighboring adults watched children play while they sat on their marble steps.

One day my grandmother took me to the neighborhood public market to do some shopping. As we walked inside, I noticed an elderly woman with gray hair sitting at the counter drinking beer and smoking a cigarette. I was shocked to see a woman of her age doing such a horrible thing. I turned to my grandmother and said, "Grandma that old lady is drinking and smoking." My grandmother looked down at me with a smile and said in her soft voice, "Honey she can drink and smoke if she wants to." I rebutted her by saying "You don't drink, or smoke and you are old." My grandmother just laughed, but I felt misunderstood. My nine years of wisdom was very much shaken that an elderly woman would drink and smoke, it just was not right. Thinking about that encounter reminded me of the cartoon called *Bobby's World*. The cartoon character portrayed a little boy with an overzealous imagination that interpreted situations in life and figurative speech with literal childlike understanding. That's how I felt in the situation with my grandmother. From my vantage point, all elderly gray-haired women should never drink nor smoke because my grandmother didn't. My grandmother was my role model, and her Christian values impacted my life greatly. They still do today.

My grandmother understood the importance of prayer and having a Savior. Early Sunday mornings, she would wake me for Sunday School. I would run to and from church for Sunday School. No one in my family went to church with me. They didn't have to because in my heart, I knew I needed Jesus Christ in my life. The stories I heard at church about Jesus Christ were very interesting. The crafts we made brought the Bible stories to life for me. The more I went to Sunday School the more I believed Jesus Christ was my Savior. My faith in Jesus Christ heightened and allowed me to fear, revere, and have a relationship with Almighty God. I did not know my heart was being transformed at that time. In fact, it wasn't until later in life that I would fully surrender my life completely to Jesus Christ by confessing, "Jesus is Lord," and believing in my heart that God raised him from the dead according to Romans 10:9. Committing my life to Jesus Christ would become the joy of my life; joy I didn't know I would desperately need.

While I was at church, my grandparents cooked Sunday brunch. Their menu was homemade applesauce, biscuits, fried chicken, and different types of vegetables. I looked forward to those meals after Sunday School. One Sunday after church I overheard my grandmother talking to my father about his alcohol problem. He would always deny it, but the truth was both of my parents drank alcohol while we lived at my grandparent's home, but never in their home. When my mother drank alcohol, she would become verbally and physically abusive towards me. Late one night, as my mother and I were returning home from visiting a family member, my mother's alcoholic rage was on full display. As we were walking down the street toward my grandparents' house, I could see the dining room window I would fondly look out of to see the neighbors' dogs. I don't know why we stopped just before we reached my grandparents' house, but suddenly my mother grabbed me and began banging my body violently against the chain link fence. The force of each impact was very hard and very painful. I was scared and I began to cry.

My grandfather must have seen us or heard my cry because he ran out of the house and stopped my mother from attacking me. He took me into the house, but refused to let my mother enter. I don't know where she went that night, but when she returned home the next day nothing was said about the incident. . . at least not in front of me. The bruises I had from the attack took a while to heal. My mother never apologized for her terrible treatment towards me. She was drunk when it happened, so she may not have remembered, and I was simply too afraid to mention it.

At ten years old, my life took a drastic turn for the worse. My father got a job and my family moved from my grandparents' house into our own home. I was incredibly sad to leave the love, comfort, and safety of my grandparents' home. When we moved, I no longer attended Sunday School. I reiterate, my mother and father were a dysfunctional couple. There were times when my mother was drinking, she would attack my father for no reason and vice versa. When they violently fought each other, I would run to my bedroom, shut my door, and put my pillow over my head. I tried to block out the yelling, screaming, and cursing, as bodies hit furniture or the floor. Her drunken wrath was not only directed towards my father. When intoxicated, my mother would beat me, pull out my hair, curse at me, and sometimes lock me out of the house for no reason. She spewed out many hurtful and damaging words when she was drunk.

Compared to the bliss of my grandparents' home, life for me was repugnant for a very long time. From the age of ten until I was thirteen years old, my father sexually molested me. At first, it seemed to be a symptom of his alcoholism, but he eventually started doing it when he was sober as well. My mother would be passed out in a drunken stupor or inexplicably not home when my father would come into my room, take me into his bedroom, or at times to the janitor's office where he worked to sexually molest me. He did things to me that are unspeakable. His ugly, coarse, big hands were rough against my skin. He made me touch places on him that I knew that I shouldn't. I will not be explicit in describing every painful and sordid moment in detail of the molestation. The word "molestation" says it all. My parents' depraved hearts had become so full of sin, they acted out their despicable sinful thoughts to my detriment.

Beyond the sexual and physical abuse I suffered at the hands of my parents was the sheer embarrassment associated with being their child. I can't count the number of times our gas and electric was turned off. My father would give my mother money to pay the utility bills, but she would spend the money on something else. I never understood why my father didn't just pay the bill himself. It was so embarrassing to approach our dark house at night. Our neighbors' lights were on, but our house stood dark and cavernous. It was especially embarrassing in the summer months when people were outside late at night sitting on their front porch. Other houses were brightly lit, and our house was dark . . . completely dark. During school months when the gas and electric was turned off, I had to go to school with wrinkled clothes because there was no electricity to press them. Every day I would buy ice from the corner store to fill the ice chests used to keep our food cold until our gas and electric was restored. People knew what was going on, they knew why my clothes were wrinkled and why I bought ice every day and it completely embarrassed me.

As if to add insult to injury, my mother would wake me up on Saturday mornings to go to the neighbor's house to borrow cigarettes for her. This was something that I hated to do. Saturday mornings were the times I did not have to go to school, and I should have been able to sleep late or watch cartoons, but I had to go beg for cigarettes for my mother. In hindsight, it was a blessing in disguise. Because of what my mother made me do, I never developed a desire to smoke cigarettes.

There were times when my parents' dysfunction surfaced outside the home. On several occasions, my father would send my mother by taxi to her mother's house when she was drinking. She stayed there until she got sober. There were times, he sent me along with her. My maternal grandmother's home was a small two-bedroom house which always seemed to be crowded with family members. If my mother became abusive toward me while we were there, my older cousins would step in to stop her from hitting me. This happened on many occasions and sometimes my mother and other family members would have physical altercations with each other.

Another embarrassing moment of public dysfunction occurred when I was walking to the store in the middle of the day for ice. There, drunk and passed out on the sidewalk, I was shocked to find my father. We were only a block away from our house, yet there he was, on the sidewalk asleep in a seated position with his back leaning against the wall of someone's home. He was so drunk he could not make it a block to his home. As people walked by, they shook their heads at the sight. While I was trying to wake my father, a neighbor drove by and stopped his car. He picked up my father's heavy body, put him in the back seat of his car, told me to get in, drove us down the street, and parked the car in front of his house. We lived three doors away from him. I opened the back door of the car to try to wake my father, but the neighbor told me, "Leave him there, when he sobers up, he will find his way home." I went to my house and, later that afternoon, my father indeed found his way home. Once again nothing was ever said about the incident, at least not in front of me.

I have a vague memory of my elementary school years. However, I clearly remember my junior and high school years. My outlet was going to school. I enjoyed reading, walking to school with my friends and just being at school. Even though I suffered abuse at home, I was blessed to be able complete my assignments and make good grades. I lived in two worlds at the time. I hid my *soul pain* from my teachers, classmates, family, and friends. Amid times of abuse, I went to school with bruises and even a black eye. In junior high school, if anyone would ask about my bruises, my excuse would be that "*I fell or walked into something.*" I portrayed myself to be very clumsy to cover the abuse. My family was very poor and sometimes I had to make sugar or mayonnaise sandwiches for lunch at school. I did not feel awkward because there were other classmates that had the same type of sandwiches. I was just thankful to have something to eat.

There were bright times between the periods of abuse. I have fond memories of my grandmother's Sunday visits to my home. She would ride the public transit bus with two large shopping bags full of my favorite homemade foods: her biscuits, applesauce, and fried chicken. She traveled by bus to come to our house until she was no longer physically able to do so. She was a selfless woman who always thought of others before herself.

Confused, embarrassed, and abused, I lost my innocence early. When innocence is lost so early, it is often replaced with something else – anger, bitterness, identity issues. My innocence was replaced with pain, *soul pain*. I did not know how to articulate it then. I knew the way my parents were treating me was wrong. Many times, I felt dirty and disgusting. The two people who were supposed to love me the most, *my parents*, were the ones abusing and hurting me the most. Who could defend me from the people assigned to protect me? I did not call the police to report the abuse. I was too afraid to run away. I had no place to go and I could not tell anyone. There was no social media to blog about my abuse. I could never tell a living soul what my mother and father were doing to me. I believed if my grandmother found out what I was going through, it would break her heart. All I knew was when my mother cursed at me, physically attacked me, or my father sexually abused me, the pain was excruciating. The pain I experienced was real. It affected me mentally, physically, emotionally, and spiritually, but I was not able to name the pain, identify what I was experiencing, or explain why it was necessary for me to endure it. I had no way of understanding the type of pain I was dealing with, but the pain was deep in my soul.

There was something else deep in my soul too . . . a knowledge of God. Thankfully, the trials I went through brought me closer to Jesus Christ. The Bible says, "The LORD is close to the brokenhearted and saves those who are crushed in spirit" (Psalm 34:18). No matter what trials I went through in life, I called on God and He heard me. Even in times when there was no response or I was too weak to believe He cared, I still believed in Him. Deep in my heart I knew there was nothing hidden from God. I knew He was aware of my plight, so I prayed incessantly for Jesus Christ to deliver me from my afflictions. Even with innocence lost and pain my constant companion, I pursued God.

I lost my innocence in my youth, but that's when my spiritual journey as a Christian began – during the darkest and most devastating times of my life. The troubles in my life were a secret between me and Jesus Christ. I would be lying if I did not admit, at times, *soul pain* was so overwhelming it overshadowed the presence of Jesus Christ in my life. My heart ached and I wondered did Almighty God's heart ache as well. The cruel words, physical beatings, inappropriate touching, and sexual molestation caused invisible scars in my heart. There was nothing I could do to prevent what was happening to me. My reality was a cesspool of sin. What I experienced by the hands of my parents was intolerable. Later in life I would read, "The heart is deceitful above all things, and desperately wicked: who can know it?" (Jeremiah 17:9) and know these choices were my parents' alone. They were the guilty party – not me, not God. However, I was left with the scars. I was left with the pain.

Fortunately, I was able to deal with the pain without displeasing God. As I've gotten older and wiser I can identify what it is – *soul pain.* For years, I held my *soul pain* in my secret closet. It was a pain the world could not know about. In this way, Satan tried to use my *soul pain* to destroy me. Thankfully, this is the type of pain only Almighty God can cure. I had to remember that God would fight my battles. The Bible says, "The LORD will fight for you; you need only to be still" (Exodus 14:14).

Soul pain continued to be difficult pain to bear for many years of my life, but because of it I gained a priceless relationship with Jesus Christ. My divine blessing of faith blossomed and grew. As I got older, I realized other people experienced *soul pain* as well. To my surprise God would use my *soul pain* for my good. The Bible says, "And we know that in all things God works for the good of those who love him, who have been called according to his purpose" (Romans 8:28). For a long time, I suffered *soul pain* in silence. I was a silent sufferer. But I will be no longer because I realize sharing my deliverance has the potential to bring about someone else's freedom.

Chapter 2

A Look In the Mirror

"I praise you because I am fearfully and

wonderfully made;

your works are wonderful;

I know that full well". (Psalms 139:14)

ﻋﻋﻋﻋﻋﻋ

"Fearfully and wonderfully made" is how David described God's making of mankind. After enduring the agonizing afflic- tion of my parents' abuse, "fearfully and wonderfully made" was certainly not how I viewed myself. What happened to me between the ages of 10 and 13 made it impossible for me to see anything within me that resembled beauty. Indeed, for a period, it was difficult to even look in a mirror. Each time I looked into a mirror; the mirror became my enemy – it caused me pain. The reflection I saw was not something I cared to see. I remember the many times I intentionally avoided looking in the mirror as I washed my hands. I was that unhappy, and the mirror reminded me of my abuse as it reflected insecurity, unattractiveness, spir- itual brokenness, and darkness in my soul. The mirror reflected *soul pain* only my eyes could see. The Bible says, "The eye is the lamp of the body. If your eyes are healthy, your whole body will be full of light" (Matthew 6:22). In *soul pain*, I felt I could not honestly display any good spiritual light, but I believed if I looked hard enough into my own eyes, I could see the hurt in the depth of my soul.

In this way, Satan tried to use my eyes to destroy me. I was not deceived by the powerful "lust of the eye" we read about in 1 John 2:16. Instead of the vanity and conceit caused by the lust of the eye, I saw loneliness and brokenness. When I looked in the mirror, I despised what I saw because I did not see an individual of worth or elegance. I was in spiritual warfare at its best, but I was also naïve as to how to engage in spiritual warfare. I'd hear people talk about it at church, but I didn't know what it meant, nor did I have the wisdom or ability to stand against the strategies of a spiritual battle. Because of my youth, I did not understand that life was both spiritual and physical and that circumstances impacted both. However, I did understand that warfare was a military battle between foes and that spiritual warfare was an invisible battle between forces of good and evil. The Bible says, "…. Do not fear or be dismayed because of this great multitude, for the battle is not yours but God's" (2 Chronicles 20:15). Yes, God would fight for me, but I needed to understand the forces responsible for this battle. My battle with *soul pain* was created by the external force of the abuse my parents delivered and the internal force of Satan's attacks on my soul.

The *soul pain* caused by my parents is evident. They were the external force at war with my soul. I did not like the family God gave me. Sure, I pretended my life was ok even though it was not. Even though I wanted to be someone else or be anywhere else, I was able to keep my emotions and abuse hidden from the world. But my heart was heavy with hurt from *soul pain*. I wondered why God allowed me to endure such horrible abuse. I heard how God loved me from my grandmother and in Sunday School, but many times, I did not feel loved. I missed out on a close relationship with my parents and I missed out on a normal childhood. Instead, my childhood and my childhood home were full of evident despair. That is not what a home should be. A home should be a stable and secure place away from the pressures of the world. Conversely, love and security were only imagined in my home and the instability in my home caused instability within my soul.

Internally, Satan's goals were evident in my life. His goals were to: become the master of my soul; destroy my relationship with God; destroy my relationship with my parents; and use *soul pain* as a deception to destroy my soul and confuse my mind in the process. The Bible says, "The thief comes only to steal and kill and destroy…." (John 10:10).   Satan delighted in confusing my mind to blind me to the wonderful human being God created me to be. My identity was in crisis as he tried to steal, kill, and destroy it. I felt alone and could see no beauty in my brokenness. Physical, mental, and spiritual pain caused false thoughts which exaggerated my self-image. The enemy of doubt and chaos had entered my mind and tricked me into believing the reflection I saw in the mirror was a flawed image. Satan tried to usurp my self-worth, appearance, and spiritual devotion to make me think I was worthless, unattractive, and unloved by anyone – including God. I unwittingly presumed that the lies Satan was feeding my mind were true. My heart and mind were disoriented, and my spiritual life was at war with evil.

I was ill prepared to win a spiritual battle with Satan or a physical battle with my parents. There was no way in my own strength I could win the spiritual battle in my mind to see the wonderful and fearful creature God made in me instead of the false image Satan created. Later I would learn the Bible says, "For our struggle is not against flesh and blood, but against the rulers, against the authorities, against the powers of this dark world and against the spiritual forces of evil in the heavenly realms" (Ephesians 6:12). This let me know I could not follow my feelings or emotions. Satan's tricks and deception were contrary to how I should live. The only way for me to win the battle of good and evil from the spiritual realm was by surrendering my life to Jesus Christ. Satan was my enemy and Jesus Christ was my friend. Jesus Christ was my salvation. In my weakness, Jesus Christ and His angels were my warriors on the battlefield of my mind and my soul. Satan had his agenda for my life, but God brought me out of the kingdom of darkness into the kingdom of light. Through Jesus Christ, Satan's lies did not continue to have power over me. Through Jesus Christ I received the truth of who I was as a human being. The Bible says, "the LORD gives sight to the blind, the LORD lifts up those who are bowed down, the LORD loves the righteous" (Psalm 146:8). I prayed continuously and stood on God's Word. Jesus Christ was my defender and deliverer. His power gave me the strength to endure. His deliverance compelled me, and I just had to be obedient to God's Holy Word and walk with Jesus Christ as my companion.

As time passed, it was the gift of divine wisdom and God's Word that allowed me to validate myself as a person of worth. God created human beings so intricately in His image, in tripartite: the body, soul, and spirit. I overcame the power the mirror had over me. Overcoming *soul pain* enabled me to be comfortable whenever I looked into a mirror because I did so by standing on God's Word: I was created in the image of God. The Bible says, "So God created mankind in his own image, in the image of God he created them" (Genesis 1:27).

Eventually God the Holy Spirit allowed me to accept the person I saw in the mirror and the person God created me to be. The human body is a gift from God and for service to the Lord. The body is only to be used as an instrument of good and righteousness. Not to satisfy lustful desires. No matter what I will go through in life, the battle is not mine it's the Lord's. In my youth, Satan wanted to steal my identity, but my identity is rooted in Jesus Christ.

Chapter 3

The Turmoil That Rages Within

"No temptation has overtaken you except what is common to mankind. And God is faithful; he will not let you be tempted beyond what you can bear. But when you are tempted, he will also provide a way out so that you can endure it".

(1 Corinthians 10:13)

৵৵৵৵৵৵

When my parents were not drinking, they were normal parents. No yelling or cursing, no toxic interactions between them. In fact, when they were not drinking, our home was peaceful. My mother took care of the house and her favorite pass time was watching soap operas. After work, my father would come home to eat and watch TV, and I obeyed my parents as a child should. The only odd thing about my home was the silence. At night, when there was no conflict, the house was so quiet you could hear a pin drop. During the day, there were no sounds, loud noises or children's laughter. The joy that happens when children run, jump, and play throughout the house did not exist in our home. As their only child I was not loud by any means – partially because it simply wasn't my nature and partially because I did not want to draw any unnecessary attention to myself.

My parents never talked about their childhood, how they met, or why they married. I never knew what caused them to be so spiritually wounded and emotionally damaged. Their choice to drink alcohol was the accelerant to act out their sinful thoughts, which created a destructive atmosphere in our home. When my parents were drinking anarchy ensued. Instead of doing what was right by God, my parents fulfilled their desire to satisfy their sinful nature. The evil in their minds and hearts caused them to commit repulsive acts toward me and toward each other. Each time my father did unspeakable things to me, I felt so dirty. When my mother physically or verbally abused me, my heart was left in a valley of helplessness. At times of abuse, I wondered why my parents didn't love me. At my weakest, I thought something was wrong with me. Surely, my parents would not have done the things they did had I not done something wrong.

Like most victims, I blamed myself for the wrong in my life. Thankfully over time, God the Holy Spirit propelled me to ac-knowledge that this type of thinking was a lie from Satan. Satan is the Father of lies. He ruins relationships, the soul, the heart, the mind, and the body. My parents' lustful acts caused me to believe Satan's lies for a season. As a result, and to his delight, chaos and turmoil raged within my soul.

To maintain stable mental health, I created a false narrative of my family, I pretended I had a loving family to combat the effects of *soul pain*. I hid my *soul pain* and dealt with it the best way that I could – by denying it existed. I was amid a mighty bat-tle for my soul and life. During the day I wore an invisible mask on my face so that no one could see my pain. It was all a façade, but to the world I appeared to be okay. Therefore, I was a nice, sweet, "happy" little girl. I was an obedient daughter, a good granddaughter, a good cousin, and a good friend. I could not let the world know my misery. I could not bring any shame upon my grandmother because of my *soul pain*. My foremost concern was my grandmother's happiness and wellbeing. I had to make sure no pain came to her because of what I was going through. I could not disclose to her that her youngest son was a child molester. Neither could I reveal that I was being physically and verbally abused by my mother. I tried to be the person my grandmother would be proud of by living righteously before God. I lived a tumultuous balancing act for three very dark years. The mental and emotional turmoil I went through was frightening.

Eventually, I could no longer ignore the reality of spiritual warfare I was facing. Miserably for a season, in the silence of the night, I could hear a loud internal roaring within my soul. The sound was silent to the ears of others, but for me the sound was deafening and set my soul on, what I perceived to be, inextinguishable fire. I heard two voices vying to control my life. One voice had good intentions and the other was for evil. Both God the Holy Spirit and Satan spoke to me simultaneously. Both *soul pain* and God the Holy Spirit were present in my soul. The spiritual part of me grappled in the battle of *soul pain* as spiritual warfare raged inside. Many times, I verbally talked myself out of responding to the pain with sinful intentions and unrighteous thoughts or actions. I knew sin was an abomination that the Lord hates. My spirit was broken, and I was desperate for divine healing. In my desperation, my broken spirit chose to be receptive of the voice of God the Holy Spirit to guide my life, the good voice.

Because of my youth, I dealt with a spiritual matters through childlike faith. God the Holy Spirit guided me to do what was right to address my *soul pain*. I constantly prayed that the abuse would end. I had to rely on God's Word day and night, along with trusting and being led by God the Holy Spirit. I was extremely limited in the knowledge of the Holy Scriptures, but I believed God's Word was true. As I got older, Jesus Christ did not allow me to stumble along in life with a victim's spirit. He did not allow me to develop a desire to drink my pain away. He did not allow me to abuse alcohol or develop any other compulsive addictive behavior to numb life's circumstances. Nor did He allow me to use any other means to destroy my temple of the Holy Spirit. Rebellion and pride did not rise within my soul as a defense mechanism.

Hate and anger did not fester within my heart against my parents, but *soul pain* remained in my soul. My choice of relieving agent for *soul pain* was Jesus Christ. He was the champion in my battle. I prayed desperately and diligently to keep a sound mind and a clean heart. I had to focus on Jesus Christ as my Lord and Savior because *soul pain* was trying to destroy my soul. The Bible says, "And do not fear those who kill the body but cannot kill the soul. Rather fear him who can destroy both soul and body in hell" (Matthew 10:28). Satan desired that I yield to his power and temptations, but if I did, he would lead me into a life of captivity and bondage. My spiritual and physical life would have no joy. My spiritual and physical life would be in never-ending unrest. Satan could not be my choice because I fiercely wanted to be out to the situation that I was in; therefore, I clung to God. God gave me the strength to stand firm, while going through *soul pain* and revealed Himself to be a merciful and a loving Father.

God the Holy Spirit ministered to me throughout those dark years of abuse. God's gift of grace allowed me to love and respect my parents regardless of the abuse they administered and to see them through eyes of faith. I dealt with this hidden enemy, *soul pain*, despite the fact I could neither see nor understand it as an enemy. How could a child deal with an invisible enemy and engage in spiritual warfare? The Bible says sins starts from thoughts in the mind and is fulfilled by acting on those thoughts. The Bible says, "The Lord saw that the wickedness of man was great in the earth, and that every intention of the thoughts of his heart was only evil continually" (Genesis 6:5). Therefore, first, I needed to understand that the actions of my parents were their own. I felt like Job, trusting God while going through afflictions. Job suffered turmoil within his soul by God's permission. It was hard for me to understand if God gave Satan permission to allow my parents to abuse me. But if He did, I had to trust Him. As for Job, the Bible says, "The churning inside me never stops; days of suffering confront me" (Job 30:27). Job's soul was full of turmoil and mine likewise. Also, like Job, I never blamed God for anything I was going through. God was not the cause of my *soul pain*. He loved me. My parents were the cause of my suffering.

Secondly, I needed to cling to hope. God knows that sin destroys His children. The Bible says, ".... the devil has been sinning from the beginning. For this is the reason the Son of God appeared was to destroy the devil's work" (1 John 3:8). I felt attacks of fiery spiritual spears from the god of this world. There were many nights I cried out to Jesus Christ because I wanted the pain to stop. The Bible says, "Now may our Lord Jesus Christ himself, and God our Father, who loved us and gave us eternal comfort and good hope through grace," (2 Thessalonians 2:16). God graced me to cling to hope. Hope that Jesus Christ would deliver me from this turmoil within. I leaned on Jesus Christ as my healing balm to give me peace for my anxious mind and calm my sad soul in times of turmoil. The Bible says, "Casting all your anxieties on him, because he cares for you" (1 Peter 5:7). I had to patiently wait on the LORD to deliver me. The Lord knew what I was going through and knew my heart. I had to seek His face and trust Him. There were times I doubted He heard my prayers. There were other times when I felt His presence was ever so close. Jesus Christ did not take the turmoil from me, but gradually gave me a sense of peace and hope while going through it. I could only hope things would get better so that God would be glorified. There was a renewing of my mind and I was given spiritual light for my dark soul. More importantly, trusting the Lord for deliverance from my circumstances gave me hope to face each day expecting change.

This way of thinking did not always work. In the back of my mind, I always feared the next episode of abuse by my parents. Fear is a paralyzer. Fear stifles the growth of the soul. I had cause to be afraid, but I need not fear. The Bible says, "The fear of man brings a snare, but whoever trusts in the LORD shall be safe" (Proverbs 29:25). My physical body was attacked by my parents to cause harm and injury. My soul was attacked by an unseen enemy called *soul pain*, but Jesus Christ defended my soul when I did not know how. He comforted me in my hopelessness. There was comfort in knowing that Almighty God was my heavenly Father. Comfort is what I sought. Comfort in Jesus Christ is what I was promised, but *soul pain* did not always allow comfort to be realized. *Soul pain* caused internal and external turmoil in my young life. The unspeakable joy promised could not always be grasped in the depths of *soul pain*. Attempts by Satan to confuse my mind were frequently a part of my youth. What was also constant in my life was Jesus Christ, He said He would never forsake or leave me. Whenever my mind started playing tricks on me, God the Holy Spirit was there to instruct and direct me in

God's truth and His love. Fortunately, I was blessed to have the presence of mind that Jesus Christ was always watching over me. This kept me grounded.

Finally, I needed godly boundaries to keep the turmoil within my soul restrained and godly boundaries to prevent bitterness from rising inside to take over my life. God promised that I shall be strengthened to overcome temptation. Only He knew how much I could bear. The Bible says, "in all your ways submit to him, and he will make your paths straight" (Proverbs 3:6). It was imperative that I believed that God was mighty, and He wanted the best for me. Therefore, I stayed on the path He prepared for me.

There are times in life when bad things happen and believers may ask, "Why am I going through this Lord?" instead of asking "Lord what are you trying to teach me through this?" God knows the *soul pain* that we sufferers will endure before it comes. The sufferer must be sensitive to the teaching and leading of God the Holy Spirit because they reveal the Father. God the Holy Spirit will continue to change the sufferer into the likeness of Jesus Christ and in doing so, the turmoil within will decrease and gradually there will be peace only Jesus Christ can give.

Chapter 4

The Mind of Jesus Christ

"In your relationships with one another,

have the same mindset as Christ Jesus".

(Philippians 2:5)

❧❧❧❧❧❧

Not only did Satan try to use my eyes to destroy me, but he also tried to use my mind to kill me. One horrible night after being molested, *soul pain* brought me to the lowest point in my life. I ran into my bedroom crouched down in a corner of the room and cried. At that moment, I felt there was no reason to hope things would ever change. Through tears, I looked at the big picture window in my bedroom and thought to myself, "All I have to do is jump out of that window, fall onto some sharp object in the yard, and kill myself." My young mind thought it would be so simple, so easy. I would be out of my misery. My father could not hurt me again. I would no longer have to live through the vile and inhumane treatment I suffered at the hands of each of my parents. The thoughts encroached my mind and nearly persuaded me to end it all.

That night is the clearest memory I have of the desire to end my life; however, these vile thoughts happened on more than one occasion. Profound suicidal thoughts persisted and were magnified when I was being physically abused or molested. My young mind and heart struggled with sad thoughts and feelings. I am so grateful when those thoughts arose, an inner voice would always caution me about committing such a heinous act. I thought to myself "How could I do such a thing? What would God think of me if I committed suicide? How could I disappoint my grandmother by thinking about killing myself? You know better than to go against the will of God." Simultaneously, my young mind thought "I am a child of God, He is my heavenly Father, I should not be going through any abuse." My child's mind believed God's children should never suffer.

The mind of a child is a fragile thing; therefore, it should not come as a surprise that *soul pain* affected my mind. Dealing with *soul pain* and not being able to confide in another human being caused mental turmoil. I was not fully aware of the scriptures about righteousness, who I was in Jesus Christ, or how evil thoughts affected my mind. Through the storms of abuse, my thoughts and heart could not fully grasp the promises of God. My mind was constantly being challenged. I battled in my mind about not disappointing God. I fought with thoughts of disappointing my grandmother. I contended with *soul pain*'s insistent thoughts of acting on my despair. As I fought the battle in my mind to remain sane, I would have conversations with Jesus Christ about the circumstances, I prayed for deliverance, and to be kept humble.

Spiritual warfare was ever-present in my mind and soul. Satan tried to rob me of a stable mental capacity, but God promised me a sound mind. The Bible says, "For God hath not given us the spirit of fear; but of power, and of love, and of a sound mind" (2 Timothy 1:7). At times, I became faint and spiritually weak trying to fight against the powerful foe of spiritual warfare in my mind. As a child all I knew was my mind had to stay focused on the things of heaven. Later, I would learn that the Bible says, "Set your minds on things that are above, not on things that are on earth" (Colossians 3:2). The negative occurrences in my life were beyond my control, but I could control my own thinking. Further, the Bible says, "Call to me and I will answer you and tell you great and unsearchable things you do not know" (Jeremiah 33:3). In Sunday School I'd heard about receiving guidance and wisdom from God. I'd heard about having the mind of Christ. I needed God the Holy Spirit's guidance to become spiritually wise and spiritually strong. I needed God the Holy Spirit's guidance to understand the meaning of having the mind of Jesus Christ and instruct me in righteous living.

What does it mean "to have the mind of Jesus Christ?" I asked myself, "Can a child have the mind of Jesus Christ or is it only for older people? How can I have the mind of Jesus Christ through my abuse?" Being spiritually naïve, I could not reasonably or wisely answer those questions, but God the Holy Spirit revealed the truth of God to me on my childish level. To have a mind of Jesus Christ is to daily remove sinful thoughts from my mind and replace them with Godly thoughts. Over time, I received the mind of Jesus Christ when dealing with my own issues in life, dealing with others, and having the desire to do the will of God. With this definition, I did the best I could to please Jesus Christ by focusing my thoughts. The Bible says, "Do not conform to the pattern of this world, but be transformed by the renewing of your mind. Then you will be able to test and approve what God's will is — his good, pleasing and perfect will" (Romans 12:2).

The power of right thinking is transformative. It takes a life-altering spiritual phenomenon to be able to think, talk, and walk in righteousness. The battle for my soul began in my mind. For this reason, it was important for me to stay focused on Jesus Christ by yielding to the leading of God the Holy Spirit. The Bible says, "We demolish arguments and pretentions that sets itself up against the knowledge of God, and we take captive every thought to make it obedient to Christ" (2 Corinthians 10:5). Taking every thought to be obedient to Jesus Christ is the beginning of wisdom and righteousness. Through God the Holy Spirit, a disciplined mind results in divine thinking.

While Jesus Christ was on earth He thought and did the things that pleased His Father in heaven. He and the Father are One; therefore, earthly pleasures had no bearing on Him because He created and controlled all things above, below, and within the earth. His mind was always set on righteousness. Having the mind of Jesus Christ requires believers to set their mind on righteousness; believe in God's Word; and apply God's Word to every decision made in life every day. Through His written Word, God provides the way to have a mind like His Son and to be changed on the inside. Jesus Christ is the only example for the Christian sufferer desirous of a sound mind. With humility, having the mind of Jesus Christ gives believers spiritual discernment to see life through eyes of faith.

The Bible says, "I can do all things through Christ who strengthens me" (Philippians 4:13). For me to do all things through Jesus Christ was a major task. God the Holy Spirit had to give me mental clarity. That clarity came as I rehearsed the moment I saw Jesus Christ being nailed to the cross. This moment not only began my journey of Christian faith, but it also gave me an image of the suffering savior who could relate to my suffering on a level no one else ever could. Hearing the Word of God in Sunday School began the renewal of my mind. I was taught in Sunday School that God always honors His Word which meant that after I'd suffered a while I'd be "perfect, established, strengthened, and settled" (1 Peter 5:10).

The Bible says "…..I know the things that come into your mind, every one of them" (Ezekiel 11:5). It is amazing to know that God knows EVERY thought that will come to the mind. Think about how many thoughts you have in a day and God knows every one of them before they come to mind. This is awesome. Consequently, it is important to have the mind of Jesus Christ to be able to think rightly. God the Holy Spirit guided me to have the mind of Jesus Christ. Having the mind of Jesus Christ did not change my circumstances, but it gave me the ability to see events in life clearer. Having the mind of Jesus Christ enabled me to discern spiritual thoughts and understand that every thought that comes into the mind is not beneficial. Thoughts of sinful acts can be redirected into righteous thoughts that will please Jesus Christ. It is important to always think what is right and pleasing in the eyes of God. Having the mind of Jesus Christ is the only way to spiritual thinking.

Chapter 5

The Godhead

"and in Christ you have been brought to fullness. He is the head
over every power and authority". (Colossians 2:10)

తతతతతత

Over the years I have often been asked how I survived such a
horrendous childhood. The fact is, during those harrowing years,
God the Holy Spirit became my pain-relieving agent in overcoming *soul pain* by revealing Jesus Christ to me. Remember when
I shared my experience of watching "The Greatest Story Ever
Told?" On that warm spring evening, I didn't realize it then, but
my spiritual journey began. God the Holy Spirit dwelled within
my heart and became my teacher by communicating with me on
a level I could understand. My life depended on the truths He
impressed within my heart. As a child I did not have the knowledge or the vocabulary to explain what I knew, but I knew God
the Holy Spirit was with me even in my most desperate moments. Now that I am older, let me explain exactly what it means
for God the Holy Spirit to be with you and how this truth got me

through the *soul pain* I suffered in my early childhood and adolescent years.

To truly understand the work of God the Holy Spirit, you have to understand the awesomeness of Almighty God's extraordinary divine nature and the individuality of the distinct personalities of the Godhead. The Godhead is composed of God the Father, God the Son, and God the Holy Spirit. Each aspect of the Godhead has His own personhood while simultaneously existing as the one and only Almighty God. The Godhead works together in harmony in all issues of human life. The Godhead was an integral part of: 1) the creation of this world; 2) the creation and existence of mankind; 3) the plan of salvation for humanity which leads to eternal life; and 4) Jesus Christ's 2nd coming to reign in the world.

All Mighty God (which is 1st in the divine nature of the Godhead) is immutable and mighty in power. He is co-eternal with God the Son and God the Holy Spirit. The Bible says, "There is no one holy like the LORD; there is no one besides you; there is no Rock like our God" (1 Samuel 2:2).

Jesus Christ (the 2nd in the divine nature of the Godhead) is the Word of God that became flesh and is co-eternal with Almighty God and God the Holy Spirit. God loves us beyond what we could ever imagine or deserve. He took the risk of revealing Himself through nature and by His Son Jesus Christ. In other words, Jesus Christ made an invisible God visible. The Bible says, "The Son is the image of the invisible God, the firstborn over all creation" (Colossians 1:15). The authority Jesus Christ displayed in the earth through miracles, signs and wonders reveals that He and the Father are one. On the surface, each miracle Jesus Christ performed was looked upon with amazement, but each had a deeper spiritual meaning. Illustrating the glory of God, each miracle Jesus Christ performed while on earth was evidence of His power over sin, nature, Satan, sickness, and death. The miracles also emphasized God's omnipotence and denounced the culture of the time Jesus Christ walked the earth.

(Each of His miracles are explained in detail in Charles C. Ryrie, "The Miracles of Our Lord." The greatest miracles were: 1) God's Word becoming a living soul; and 2) the miracle of Jesus Christ's precious blood shed as the redemption and salvation of all humanity. The latter miracle did not only occur the moment of Jesus Christ's death on the cross, but this miracle of redemption and salvation continues each day. Jesus Christ is both the offering and the offeror of salvation. Acts 4:12 says, "Salvation is found in no one else, for there is no other name under heaven given to mankind by which we must be saved."

God the Holy Spirit is third in the divine nature of the Godhead and is co-eternal with Almighty God the Father and Jesus Christ, God the Son. God the Holy Spirit is a gift given to all believers by the Father through Jesus Christ. God the Holy Spirit is the spirit of Almighty God living inside the hearts of God's children. God the Holy Spirit is sweet, loving, caring and guides God's children in ways of uprightness. Upon a believer's spiritual birth, Jesus Christ asks the Heavenly Father to send a teacher, a sanctifier and helper in all spiritual things to His children. God lovingly sends this divine gift in the person of God the Holy Spirit.

God the Holy Spirit powerfully persuades, changes hearts and minds, and deposits every Word of God into the heart of every believer. In John 14:16, Jesus says, "And I will ask the Father, and he will give you another advocate to help you and be with you forever." In John 15:26, Jesus goes on to say, "But when the Helper comes, whom I shall send to you from the Father, the Spirit of truth who proceeds from the Father, He will testify of Me."

During the years of abuse, I experienced exactly what Jesus described. A sickening feeling would always creep into my stomach when my parents were drunk. In the back of my mind, I wondered what abuse I would endure that night. I felt so overwhelmed with *soul pain* that my spirit was lost to my circumstances. The trepidation associated with potentially being abused caused me to feel like crawling into a hole, covering it, and never coming out. In spite the years of abuse, I was able to experience exactly what Jesus described in John 15:26. Jesus Christ sent me the helper to comfort and strengthen me to bear my burdens. My helper drew me closer to Jesus Christ as I endured *soul pain*. The helper dwelt in the secret place in my heart and spoke to me. In my youth, God the Holy Spirit spoke to me very sweetly and quietly. He ministered to my mind, heart, and soul. I was too young to understand what was happening in my spiritual life, but I was coming to know God through my *soul pain*.

As my faith grew, so did my understanding. In my youth, I was naïve to the role of the Godhead and how it impacted *soul pain* in my life. I was unaware of the Godhead's efficacious power in the world and within the believer. It is true, Believers can never live up to the standards of Almighty God, especially in *soul pain* because human beings are imperfect and have a sin nature. However, Jesus Christ covers those imperfections, and makes His children acceptable and pleasing before a Holy God. The Bible says, "In this is love, not that we have loved God but that he loved us and sent his Son to be the propitiation for our sins" (1 John 4:10). Each person of the Godhead imparts His astonishing character and power. Each tenderly pours out His unconditional love, empathy, and goodness. What a beautiful mystery?

Surprisingly, God the Holy Spirit allowed me to recognize that my parents were tools used by Satan to try to destroy my soul. On more than one occasion, He cautioned me of two things I still remember today, "Do not take on your parents' sin" and "I will make your enemies your footstool." These were powerful directives. I did not understand what those statements meant at the time. I was not sure if I was just imagining those words in my mind, or if God was really speaking to me at all. *Soul pain* reigned, but the desire to do what was right before Almighty God reigned as well. Years later I understood what those words meant. Attributable to my grandmother's prayers and prayers of my own, God the Holy Spirt convicted me of my sin and convinced me to have faith in Jesus Christ. God the Holy Spirit instructed me not to give up because of my circumstances or yearn to live the ungodly lifestyle of my parents.

Believers must realize and believe they are crucified, raised, and have new life IN Jesus Christ. As believers begin to understand who they are IN Jesus Christ they will also begin to truly understand how to live in this world in good times, heartache, and pain while being prepared for the life hereafter. The Bible says, "Therefore if any man be IN Christ, he is a new creature: old things are passed away; behold, all things are become new" (2 Corinthians 5:17). Surrendering a life to Jesus Christ is the best decision a person could ever make.

As a young immature Christian, spiritual wisdom was hard for me to comprehend. Life IN Jesus Christ was difficult for me to discern. Through *soul pain*, my soul yearned to be loved even when things were at their worst. Day by day, God the Holy Spirit gently encouraged me to live life IN Jesus Christ. God the Holy Spirit ultimately made me receptive of spiritual things in heaven, love for Almighty God, having faith in Jesus Christ, and trusting in God the Holy Spirit. Later in my life, I concluded and believed that my life was not about me, but about worshipping and glorifying God in all that I think, say, and do. Being a new creature IN Jesus Christ, caused me to want to live by new principles which allowed love to flow out of my new heart. To be IN Jesus Christ is to have my sins forgiven. To be IN Jesus Christ is to have His mind of discernment. To be IN Jesus Christ is to have God the Holy Spirit dwelling within my heart. To be IN Jesus Christ means my pain was His pain. To be IN Jesus Christ means I have His righteousness. To be IN Jesus Christ means I have eternal life. To be IN Jesus Christ means I am His work of art. The Bible says, "I have been crucified with Christ. It is no longer I who live, but Christ who lives in me. And the life I now live in the flesh I live by faith in the Son of God, who loved me and gave himself for me" (Galatians 2:20). I am so grateful that God the Holy Spirit dwells within my spiritual heart. Dependence on God the Holy Spirit was essential for my continual connection with God the Father.

There are many misconceptions about the identity of God the Holy Spirit. Some view God the Holy Spirit as a mystical force out there somewhere. Some believe God the Holy Spirit is an impersonal power that God makes available to followers of Jesus Christ and some ignore the existence of God the Holy Spirit altogether. The Bible declares that God the Holy Spirit is God. God the Holy Spirit, the spirit of God, was my guide to know the truth about Almighty God and Jesus Christ. The Bible says, "so that Christ may dwell in your hearts through faith. And I pray that you, being rooted and established in love" (Ephesians 3:17).

Being part of God's family, promises an intimate relationship with the Godhead and the divine truth is established in the heart, mind, and soul of the believer.

I was blessed to hear a soft, quiet voice, speak to me in times of trouble to calm my unhappy soul. Had I not obeyed the instructions of God the Holy Spirit; my life could have taken a different course. I followed His instruction. It empowered me to do what was right. God the Holy Spirit taught me to have faith in Jesus Christ. God the Holy Spirit sensitized me of the corrupt sinful nature of my parents as well as my own corrupt nature. The Bible says, "But when he, the Spirit of truth, comes, he will guide you into all the truth. He will not speak on his own; he will speak only what he hears and he will tell you what is yet to come" (John 16:13). God the Holy Spirit is my close confidante that I cherish, love, and adore. He affectionately and patiently guided me through many effects of *soul pain*, while developing my relationship with the Godhead and teaching me the meaning of being a child of God. A biblical world view is manifested when the sinner becomes a child of God.

Chapter 6

Peace That Transcends Understanding

"Peace I leave with you; my peace I give you. I do not give to you as the world gives. Do not let your hearts be troubled and do not be afraid". (John 14:27)

❧❧❧❧❧❧

After two years of appalling abuse by my parents, one dark night of mental anguish, I went into my bedroom, laid down on my bed and began to cry and cry out to the Lord. Suddenly a feeling of divine peace came over me. The Bible says, "And the peace of God, which transcends all understanding, will guard your hearts and your minds in Christ Jesus" (Philippians 4:7). It was a kind of peace that was mystifying to me, but conceivable to God. I never felt that sensation before. It was a feeling that is difficult to describe other than to say it was a peace that transcends understanding. It was peace from Jesus Christ, the God of Peace that gave rest to my weary soul.

That night I slept soundly and peacefully. Instead of feeling dirty or unworthy, I felt an unexpected kind of peace in my soul. That night I was given God's peace, the kind of inner peace that only comes from Jesus Christ, to combat my *soul pain*. It was as if through the maze of spiritual anarchy, Jesus Christ heard and answered my prayers. I had the peace of God and I was at peace with God. The abuse did not stop, but the divine peace I experienced began to minimize the devastating effects of *soul pain*. The Bible says, "Before they call, I will answer; while they are still speaking, I will hear" (Isaiah 65:24). As I cried that night, God heard and granted me something I could hold on to – something real. A promise of Almighty God had been released to me and I was in full possession of it.

The Bible says, "I have told you these things, so that in me you may have peace. In this world you will have trouble. But take heart! I have overcome the world" (John 16:33). In this world I did have trouble. Molestation produced the heart wrenching *soul pain* which detonated a tumultuous rumbling deep within the crevices in my soul. Like a wild river scars a landscape, tears of pain flowed down my face and scarred my heart. Many nights *soul pain* caused me to be on bended knees urgently and desperately pleading to Jesus Christ to remove the pain and give me peace in my soul. I wondered on many occasions "why was I was going through this agony," but I still refused to blame God for my suffering.

In times of *soul pain*, the only alternative I had was to cast my burdens on the Lord Jesus Christ and He answered my prayers. The Bible says, "Now may the Lord of peace himself give you peace at all times in every way….." (2 Thessalonians 3:16). The peace God gives is how you overcome the world. True heavenly peace can only be found in Jesus Christ. Just as agape love is Almighty God Himself, divine peace is Jesus Christ Himself. Through Jesus Christ I was given His peace. *Soul pain* caused me great distress, but divine peace gave me the ability to stay calm in distressful times. I had faith in the Lord Jesus Christ, and it was He who gave me hope that the abuse would end.

Soul pain and God's peace are polar opposites. *Soul pain* brings agony and confusion, whereas God's peace brings joy and well-being. When there is chaos all around, the believer can have the peace Jesus Christ brings, assurance, and self-control. I am grateful to have had the peace of Jesus Christ, while going through *soul pain*. The Bible says, "Praise be to the God and Father of our Lord Jesus Christ, the Father of compassion and the God of all comfort, who comforts us in all our troubles" (2 Corinthians 1:3-4). I sought a calmness for my soul and received comfort IN my trouble. The time I felt divine peace, I realized I was not alone in my *soul pain*. It was at the point of my worst hurt that I realized Jesus Christ was closest to me. The Bible says, "Consider it pure joy, my brothers and sisters, whenever you face trials of many kinds, because you know that the testing of your faith produces perseverance. Let perseverance finish its work so that you may be mature and complete, not lacking anything" (James 1:2-4). In the midst of *soul pain*, I did not think about asking God what He was trying to teach me, but today I know I am always free to ask for the peace from God. Though it may not come when requested, the moment I reach out to God for help I am able to dwell in God's safety while waiting for peace to come.

It will forever remain a mystery as to how Divine peace was given through Jesus Christ. Divine peace amid chaos is perplexing to the world, but this kind of peace can only come by being in a right relationship with Jesus Christ. God's divine nature gives the believer His divine peace that goes beyond understanding. It is a wonderful peace that embraces the soul, washes the heart, and rescues the mind. Peace that Jesus Christ promises is not found in this world, it emerges from the heavenly realm. It is because of love from Jesus Christ, I received peace from God. Sadly, many will never encounter this type of peace in their lifetime. It is through Jesus Christ that I can be in the presence of Almighty God at any time. Because of God's peace I gained a sense of reverential fear for God's power, a deep desire to do what was right, and was deterred from willfully committing sin. I relied on Jesus Christ for peace in my soul and depended on God the Holy Spirit to live under God's divine and moral law.

Chapter 7

The Act of Forgiveness

"Be kind and compassionate to one another, forgiving each other,
just as in Christ God forgave you." (Ephesians 4:32)

ৰ্তৰ্তৰ্তৰ্তৰ্তৰ্ত

Forgiveness is dynamically twofold. First, there is divine forgiveness that God bestows upon humanity, forgiveness from the perpetual penalty of sin. God's divine forgiveness is pure because His nature and character are pure. God commissioned His Son, Jesus Christ, to save the entire world. The Bible says, "For God so loved the world, that he gave his only begotten Son, that whosoever believeth in him should not perish, but have everlasting life" (John 3:16). Jesus Christ will continually be the instrument of God's forgiveness to save unworthy people.

God demonstrated forgiveness throughout scripture. In the Old Testament God forgave Israel as a nation and forgave its people individually. The nation of Israel, God's chosen people, sinned against God numerous times, but in turn God forgave them numerous times. Israel rebelled against God in captivity and while they were free, yet God loved and forgave His chosen nation when they cried out for deliverance as a nation or individually. Take for example Exodus 32:1 which says, "When the people saw that Moses delayed coming down from the mountain, the people gathered together to Aaron, and said to him, "Come, make us gods that shall go before us; for as for this Moses, the man who brought us up out of the land of Egypt, we do not know what has become of him." In the absence of a man, God's chosen people rebelled against God, but later in that same chapter Moses intercedes on their behalf, God forgives, and restrains His wrath.

In the New Testament we find the ultimate example of forgiveness as Jesus Christ leaves the glory of heaven to come down into this fallen and depraved world to cover the sins, not just of one nation, but of the entire world. This appeasement of God's wrath was necessary because of the world's propensity towards sin. Jesus Christ came so that the world could be forgiven. His sacrificial act satisfied the wrath of God towards His sinful children and restored their relationship with God broken because of sin. This is the definitive act of forgiveness. The Bible says, "He is the propitiation for our sins, and not for ours only but also for the sins of the whole world" (1 John 2:2). God provides the sinner the only way to be forgiven once and for all. Surrendering a life to Jesus Christ is the only way to have a true relationship and eternal life with Almighty God.

Further, forgiveness is a command from Almighty God for the believer. Ephesians 4:32 says, "Be kind and compassionate to one another, forgiving each other, just as in Christ God forgave you." This is no easy feat. In fact, believers cannot truly forgive anyone without God's intercession; therefore, God the Holy Spirit is the internal force igniting the desire to forgive, the ability to forgive, and the very act of forgiveness.

No, forgiveness is not easy, but forgiveness is necessary. It is one of the divine principles of God's love and when we yield to God the Holy Spirit's influence, God grants us the ability to forgive as a gift. The gift of forgiveness is given to the believer through faith because of obedience to God. God gives the gift of forgiveness to His children to forgive themselves and forgive others. Forgiveness is the gift of release. Release absolves past wrongs committed by an offender to free the victim of past, current, or forthcoming *soul pain*. Release brings peace to the soul and to the world. As a result, no act of retaliation is executed by the victim because of a hurtful act. The act of forgiveness may need to be extended by a victim once, twice, or many times. The Bible tells us how many times the believer is to forgive. Matthew 18:21-22 says, "Then Peter came to Jesus and asked, 'Lord, how many times shall I forgive my brother or sister who sins against me? Up to seven times?' Jesus answered, 'I tell you, not seven times, but seventy-seven times." Unconditional release will ease the gnawing pang of past harm, heartache, burdens, and bondage. The offender may never ask for forgiveness, but victims are empowered through forgiveness as it brings spiritual stability into their lives. Justice may be executed, but forgiveness is required.

Believers must forgive because they have been forgiven by God. The Bible says, "In him we have redemption through his blood, the forgiveness of our trespasses, according to the riches of his grace" (Ephesians 1:7). To be an obedient child of God, the believer must obey God's commandments. Refusing to forgive someone that has harmed the believer is a sin. If harmed, the incident may never be forgotten, but it is up to God to execute judgment against the perpetrator. Having a relationship with your foe may never materialize due to an unpleasant or horrific incident, but forgiveness frees the believer of future flashbacks and the resulting/associated negative behaviors. It also frees the foe from future punishment.

Jesus Christ's grace allowed me to not have any bitterness, hate, or anger toward my parents. I was able to forgive my parents for the abuse I endured by their hands. My heart became willing to administer forgiveness to those that harmed me. Had I not forgiven my parents, they would have had power over my life, and I would not have had freedom to live past the abuse. The Bible says, "honor your father and mother, and love your neighbor as yourself" (Matthew 19:19). I was afraid to disobey the commandments of God. As I obeyed God's commandments, my relationship with Jesus Christ grew stronger, the gift of forgiveness grew stronger within me as well. Leaning on Jesus Christ gave me the courage to turn from hate and freed me from the stranglehold of depression and negative behaviors.

In 1967, my mother left the house early in the morning to go to the liquor store. While crossing the street she was struck by a car and landed on the hood of the vehicle. She had bumps, bruises, and sustained a serious head injury. Both of her retinas were detached. Her eyesight was already in poor condition due to repeated punches to her eyes because of fist fights with my father, but the accident made her eyes worse. The driver did not have car insurance; therefore, my mother was never compensated for injuries nor her pain and suffering. She was thirty-three years old.

The car accident caused my mother to have short term amnesia. She was admitted to a psychiatric hospital for the mentally ill. Initially, she did not recognize her husband or her child, but within a few months she regained her memory, and was discharged to return home. Upon her return, she could no longer do household chores or take care of her daily needs. Fortunately, she was familiar with the floorplan of our home, so it was easy for her to get around. Because of her limited eyesight, she was very restricted in the things she was able to do for herself. I had to take over all the household chores and I became my mother's caregiver. The verbal and physical abuse executed by my mother toward me had finally ended. I was thirteen years old.

Five years after the accident, I contacted the League for the Blind to utilize their services to teach my mother skills to maintain a normal life. Their services were free to those who were blind. An instructor came to the house to teach my mother to walk independently outdoors with a cane. After her first day of training, my mother refused to be trained any further. My mother was a very defiant woman. She always believed her eye condition was temporary and she would regain total eyesight at any moment. When someone would ask her how she was doing, her response would be, "I'm working on my eyes and I will be better soon". I was concerned that she was not accepting her condition. I spoke to a counselor at the League for the Blind about my mother's mental state and I was told that my mother was in denial about her eyesight. She never accepted her blindness and I never said anything to her to the contrary. I accompanied my mother to her many doctors' appointments and after several eye surgeries she was declared legally blind.

Jesus Christ allowed me to go without any resentment in my heart in exchange for forgiveness. The Bible says, "But if you do not forgive others their sins, your Father will not forgive your sins" (Matthew 6:15). The gift of forgiveness enabled me to love, serve, and appreciate others. There is an assurance in the truth of God's Word that strengthened me to carry out the attribute of forgiveness. God was sufficient to answer my prayers, to give me a heart to forgive, and the ability to withstand my burdens. The

Bible says, "This is my commandment, that you love one another as I have loved you" (John 15:12). Love, forgiveness, grace and salvation are prominent themes throughout the Bible. Forgiveness is not just something that we do for others and ourselves, but it connects us to the Godhead. The Bible says, "For if you forgive others their trespasses, your heavenly Father will also forgive you" (Matthew 6:14). Jesus Christ requests that we freely and fully forgive our enemies through our new life IN Him. Forgiveness brings control back into the life of the believer and forgiveness diminishes *soul pain* over time. I forgave those that hurt me because it is required of all Christians.

Chapter 8

Strength In God's Grace

"Grace and peace be yours in abundance through the knowledge of God and of Jesus our Lord". (2 Peter 1:2)

స~స~స~స~స~స~

Grace is magnificently twofold. First, there is unmerited sovereign grace that God bestows upon humanity. Grace is pure because it is the essence of God and He willingly gives His grace to the undeserving. The Bible says, "for all have sinned and fall short of the glory of God, and all are justified freely by his grace through the redemption that came by Christ Jesus" (Romans 3:23-24). We are justified through grace and by Jesus Christ's atonement, we are saved. Mankind cannot bestow this type of grace upon itself, upon others, or earn it. Only the love of God can perform the impossible act of extending grace to humanity; therefore, He freely gives His children what they need according to His divine grace.

In the Old Testament, Israel enjoyed God's grace because Almighty God Himself was with them. He selected them to be His chosen people who both received His Holy Word and were chosen to be living examples of God's Word to the world. No other nation was so divinely employed. In Deuteronomy 14:2, God says of Israel, "for you are a people holy to the LORD your God. Out of all the peoples on the face of the earth, the LORD has chosen you to be his treasured possession." God gave Moses the Ten Commandments and then told His nation ".... I have set before you life and death, blessings and curses. Now choose life, so that you and your children may live" (Deuteronomy 30:19). In other words, once God gave His commandments, He also gave His nation the choice to obey the commandments. Because of willful disobedience, Israel often found itself in captivity. The deliverance of Israel was the direct result of undeserved grace from Almighty God. Israel's cycle of captivity and deliverance is a picture of the sinful nature of mankind as well as the world's desperate need for grace.

In the New Testament, grace is depicted as a blessing to the undeserving. Mankind's sin nature makes it impossible to conduct the degree of good works necessary to rescue humanity from condemnation. Therefore, because of grace, Almighty God sent His only begotten Son to earth to save the lost and set the captives free. The Bible says, "For it is by grace you have been saved, through faith—and this is not from yourselves, it is the gift of God—not by works, so that no one can boast. For we are God's handiwork, created in Christ Jesus to do good works, which God prepared in advance for us to do" (Ephesians 2:8-10). Believers belong wholly to Almighty God and as new creations in Jesus Christ with a new nature, they are gifted with divine grace.

Second, the gift of grace is given to believers by a Holy God to influence the world with spiritual wisdom and compassion. Grace is given to believers to see life through the eyes of faith.

There are many circumstances in life which cause heartache and *soul pain*. Believers who live by grace through faith are equipped to overcome and even prosper in those circumstances. The Bible says, "Therefore, the promise comes by faith, so that it may be by grace and may be guaranteed to all Abraham's offspring..." (Romans 4:16).

There are different categories of grace: 1) divine grace; Almighty God commissioned His Son, Jesus Christ, to come to earth not to live like us, but to die for us; 2) supreme act of grace; that Jesus Christ carried out the on the cross for the world. This is an act of selflessness; 3) the gift of grace; believers are given this gift by Jesus Christ as inner strength to endure; and 4) extended grace; grace changes the heart of the believer to change lives of others. It is by faith that believers receive grace, and it is by faith that believers give grace. Grace granted by a believer to others is an illustration of heaven. The Bible says, "And whatever you do, whether in word or deed, do it all in the name of the Lord Jesus, giving thanks to God the Father through him" (Colossians 3:17). Those outside the faith cannot understand how or why a believer will not retaliate when harmed by a perpetrator or are able to help that perpetrator when in need. It is the gift of divine grace that can look past the faults of others and see them through eyes of love. God the Holy Spirit gives believers the power to grant kindness to insensitive and uncaring people. Through God the Holy Spirit, the believer can grant grace in the most awkward circumstances and in the most horrible situations. It is because of the divine gift of grace through Jesus Christ, hearts are changed, and minds are transformed.

It would have been extremely easy for me to become a bitter and angry person, but grace from Jesus Christ changed me in many ways. I did not like everything that happened in my life, but God's grace was the balm that healed my *soul pain* and grew my faith. Grace allowed me to see people through eyes of faith. I was able to maintain a state of grace in my heart with the help from God the Holy Spirit. I was able to grant grace to my parents without regard of past abuse. Grace made life's hardships easier for me to deal with. I chose to please my Heavenly Father, to show compassion to my earthly parents, and be kind to others. Grace gave me the fortitude not to be crushed by life's circumstances or by the sinful actions of others. Grace allowed me to survive years of evil.

Retaliating against my parents would displease God and that was something I feared because I genuinely wanted to live in my new nature. God gave me the gift of His grace to withstand hurt and pain. Further, God's grace gave me the ability to grow spiritually from that pain. Eventually, His gift of grace would provide the relief I needed to love the very people who hurt me. Grace did not absolve what was done, but grace gave me peace in my heart to understand it. I went through abuse and I am not the only person that has or will go through such agony. Had I focused on revenge against my parents or attacked others because of my pain, I would have missed God's blessings. Divinely God protected my soul from destruction and cared for me in the presence of my enemies (my parents). God's grace is still healing my heart every day.

While in the throngs of abuse, I did not understand God was bestowing His divine grace upon me, but as time went on, it was apparent that God produced more grace within me. No matter what I went through in life, God's grace was sufficient for me to endure the agony of *soul pain*. The Bible says, "You then, my son, be strengthened by the grace that is in Christ Jesus" (2 Timothy 2:1). Grace allowed me to hold on to the loving hand of God. His grace comforted me in my distress and strengthened me when I was weak. God the Holy Spirit taught me the importance of grace. Best of all, God's grace grew my relationship with Jesus Christ. God's grace also accentuated the will of God within me and forbade me to be quarrelsome or disrespect my parents. Grace awakened my soul with a desire to act properly before God. Receiving the grace of Jesus Christ was my lifeline. Grace gave me the courage to go on another day and allowed me to humbly persevere through adversities that would have easily hardened my heart. Instead, grace gave me spiritual compassion to care about others.

God has blessed the believer by His grace and His providence. God's love brings the believer comfort, joy, and His confidence to believe what is right and true. Grace is the persuader when the flesh says not to be kind because of *soul pain* as it encourages the heart to act in ways that glorify Almighty God.

Chapter 9

The Sweetness of Mercy

"Be merciful, even as your Father is merciful".

(Luke 6:36)

વ્જ્જ્જ્જ્જ્જ્જ્

Mercy is beautifully twofold. First, the highest form of mercy is a divine act of Almighty God. God's mercy is pure because He gives mercy to each generation with compassion and justice. The Bible says, "The Lord is merciful and gracious, slow to anger and abounding in steadfast love" (Psalm 103:8). The manner in which Almighty God deals with mercy can be seen in His relationship with His people in the Old and New Testaments through the act of reconciliation – the greatest act of mercy. Before the earth was formed, God planned a way for humanity to be reconciled to Him. God owes mankind nothing, but He continues to show mercy to broken human beings because He so chooses. Romans 9:15 says, "For He says to Moses, 'I will have mercy on whomever I will have mercy, and I will have compassion on whomever I will have compassion." Mercy and compassion are the flip sides of a coin.

Some believe the Old Testament describes the Almighty God as a tyrannical God of wrath who desires superficial sacrificial offerings and encourages violence by His people to receive glory. This superficial observance lacks nuance and ignores the extraordinary mercy Almighty God extends to His chosen people because of love. His acts of mercy can be seen in the Books of Genesis through Malachi. God not only showed mercy to Israel, but upon all He created. The Bible says, "The LORD is good to all, and his mercy is over all that he has made" (Psalm 145:9).

Disobedience caused the expulsion of Adam and Eve from the garden, but by God's mercy they were provided clothing to cover their nakedness, protection from the elements outside of the garden, and the meeting of their needs. According to Genesis 3:21, "The LORD God made garments of skin for Adam and his wife and clothed them." God showed mercy to Abraham and Sarah because of their years of barrenness. He promised and gave them a child to bless all the families of the earth. The Bible says, "Now the LORD was gracious to Sarah as he had said, and the LORD did for Sarah what he had promised" (Genesis 21:1). While the nation of Israel was in the wilderness and Moses was on the mountain, sadly the freed Israelites worshipped false gods and committed profane acts of sin instead of worshipping the Almighty God who freed them. How unconscionable? God was filled with anger and proclaimed destruction upon the nation of Israel because of their unbelief, wickedness, and corruption. "I have seen these people, the LORD said to Moses, and they are a stiff-necked people. Now leave me alone so that my anger may burn against them and that I may destroy them. Then I will make you into a great nation. But Moses sought the favor of the LORD his God. 'LORD,' he said, '...why should your anger burn against your people, whom you brought out of Egypt with great power and a mighty hand? Why should the Egyptians say, It was with evil intent that he brought them out, to kill them in the mountains and to wipe them off the face of the earth? Turn from your fierce anger; relent and do not bring disaster on your people. Remember your servants Abraham, Isaac and Israel, to whom you swore by your own self: 'I will make your descendants as numerous as the stars in the sky and I will give your descendants all this land I promised them, and it will be their inheritance forever.' Then the LORD relented and did not bring on his people the disaster he had threatened" (Exodus 32:9-14). Even in their disobedience God did not abandon His people. With love and mercy God sympathized and promised to do no harm. Disobedience will always occur with people, but every day God distributes His mercy.

In the New Testament, Jesus Christ's mercy can be seen through His profound power over nature, Satan, sickness, sin, life, and death. The merciful miracles Jesus Christ performed changed the world. Jesus Christ's mercy can be seen in the Gospel Books of Matthew, Mark, Luke and John through the book of Revelation. God poured out mercy to New Testament believers by pardoning their sins through Jesus Christ; thereby making Jesus Christ a gift of mercy from Almighty God as well as a giver of mercy to the world from the Roman Empire to today, and forever more. Mercy is revealed to people today, through a desired relationship with Jesus Christ. Believers receive mercy through the blood of Jesus Christ. His blood purchases the believer's bondage of sin, gives them salvation, freedom, and eternal life with Almighty God. The Bible says, "For God did not send his Son into the world to condemn the world, but in order that the world might be saved through him" (John 3:17). This mercy will be given to every believer forever.

Jesus Christ's life's work was to dispense absolute mercy. He administered mercy to the souls of men and healed their bodies. The Bible says, "Blessed are the merciful, for they will be shown mercy" (Matthew 5:7). Almighty God showed mercy in the past, present, and will forever show mercy in the future. According to Psalm 103:17 . . . "the mercy of the Lord is from everlasting to everlasting . . ." Almighty God never changes.

Second, God gives the gift of mercy as a blessing to and through His children to give mercy to others. Jesus Christ indicates that His people will be shown mercy and they must give mercy to those who are suffering instead of inflicting punishment. Believers are to emulate Jesus Christ's mercy by being loving, kind, and compassionate. The Bible says "Do not conform to the pattern of this world but, be transformed by the renewing of your mind... (Romans 12:2).

As a child, I had the presence of mind to understand that God the Holy Spirit lived within me and taught me God's truth. If I displayed any unkind behavior toward my parents and others, this behavior would not be acceptable to Jesus Christ. Kindness, mercy, and forgiveness had to be my character; however, I could not develop these characteristics alone. Hebrews 4:16 says, "Let us then with confidence draw near to the throne of grace, that we may receive mercy and find grace to help in time of need." The approach of my judgements had to come from God's Word. I had to let God be the judge of my parents' actions as well as mine. My heart chose to give mercy.

Thankfully, God gave me the gift of mercy. As a victim of maltreatment – and according to the world's standards – I should be simmering with hate, have resentment in my heart, and be riddled with low self-esteem. In fulfilling worldly standards, I should selfishly dispense anger toward anyone who harmed or mistreated me and not give mercy. Also, I should project anger toward even the innocent people in my path. If I had given over to anger, my life would have been miserable. I, not my abusers, would have been living in unhappiness. Praise God these worldly standards did not materialize in my life. Instead, the Almighty God transformed my heart and renewed my mind. I sought mercy for myself from my Heavenly Father and I chose to give mercy to my parents. God the Holy Spirit quietly and clearly spoke to my heart orchestrating mercy. As God demanded, I had to honor my parents despite the abuse. The Bible says. "Honor your father and your mother, that your days may be long in the land that the Lord your God is giving you" (Exodus 20:12).

Some people may find it difficult to understand how or why I gave my parents mercy. The reason is simple, I received mercy from God, and felt I had to give this gift to others. I could not hold grudges or seek vengeance. I had to leave my *soul pain* in God's hands. God knew about all my family's dirty secrets. He knew I was in spiritual pain – the type of pain only He could cure. The entire time I was abused by my parents, I constantly prayed and cried out to Jesus Christ to have mercy on me and to remove my *soul pain*. God the Holy Spirit would not allow me to treat my parents harshly or dishonorably. I could not break the heart of God because of my *soul pain*. I had to trust God the Holy Spirit to give me the power to give mercy. I could not execute punishment even if punishment was due.

When I was in 12th grade, my mother's disabled sister became homeless. Alcoholism had damaged her kidneys and for some unknown reason it was difficult for her to walk. She had to rely on a walker to get around. When I found out she was homeless I went to get her and moved her in with us. There was not a second thought about her moving in. Not only was I my mother's caregiver, but I became my aunt's caregiver as well. I would make sure breakfast and lunch were prepared for them before I went to school. When I got home after school, I cooked dinner. My father did his janitorial work during the day and watched TV when he came home in the evening. As time passed, my aunt's health got better, and she looked stronger. I did household chores, cared for my mother, father, and aunt as an adolescent through young adulthood. A caregiver's job is difficult, but worthwhile. The Bible says, "And God is able to make all grace abound toward you; that ye, always having all sufficiency in all things, may abound to every good work...." (2 Corinthians 9:8). I was willing to do for others to please God. Therefore, I chose to show mercy to my family members and not anger.

One day an older cousin convinced my aunt to move in with her. My aunt agreed, but that was the worst decision she could have made — she stayed at my cousin's house for a while. After another family member told me that my aunt was not well, I went to visit her. My aunt looked terrible, and my heart ached for her. She was laying in her own urine on the sofa. Without informing my cousin, I took my aunt back home with me, cleaned her up, and gradually she began to regain her strength again. Within a year her kidneys stopped functioning properly and began to fail. I took her to the hospital and was told there was nothing the doctors could do. Her kidneys were so damaged she would not benefit from dialysis. So, I brought her back home to die. My mother's older sister came over to help me bath and feed her when she could. My sick aunt's health declined very quickly. It got to the point I could not take care for her any longer. I took her back to the hospital for the last time, she died June 20, 1975. She was 45 years old.

About a year after my aunt's death, I convinced my mother to be trained to do things around the house. So, she could become independent. She agreed and was admitted into an in-house program at the MD Rehabilitation Facility for the Blind for training. By the second day I was called to come to get her and take her home because she believed they could not provide the training and care she needed. After that debacle, my mother refused any type of rehabilitation training. She never regained her eyesight. In fact, her eyes became worse and over the years she developed glaucoma and cataract eye diseases.

Humbly I did the best that I could to care for my mother and father. Mercy allowed me to forgive my parents' abuse and be kind. I showed them compassion and love when they did not deserve it. When someone hurts you, mercy is the gift believers are given to overcome an offence. The Bible says "Pay attention to yourselves! If your brother sins, rebuke him, and if he repents, forgive him, and if he sin against you seven times in the day, and turns to you seven times, saying, 'I repent,' you must forgive him" (Luke 17:3-4). It is the power of God the Holy Spirt within that puts mercy into action. God's mercy and kindness can be experienced and seen everywhere. His mercy is renewed every day. Not only is Almighty God a God of mercy, but He also expects His children to be merciful.

Chapter 10

A Servant's Heart

"I will give you a new heart and put a new spirit in you; I will remove from you your heart of stone and give you a heart of flesh".

(Ezekiel 36:26)

૬ન૬ન૬ન૬ન૬ન૬ન

Amazingly, I felt no anger or hatred toward anyone. Instead, God's divine grace and mercy gave me a new heart to serve and I lived by Jesus Christ's standard of unselfish servanthood. Jesus Christ's purpose was to do the will of His Heavenly Father over everything else. In fact, Mark 10:45 says, "For even the Son of Man did not come to be served, but to serve..." While on earth, with humility, Jesus Christ was the epitome of servanthood. Through His love, grace, teaching, preaching, and healing He demonstrated that the welfare of others was an utmost priority to Him.

By submitting my life to Jesus Christ, it became my duty to serve others without seeking anything in return. Because salvation produced in me a servant's heart, serving my family and others with love and kindheartedness seemed to be a natural part of my being. As my heart changed, my focus changed: instead of viewing service to others as a burden, I saw it as a blessing. I was grateful that God gave me the physical ability to carry out all the tasks associated with caring for my family. Indeed, it was important to me to not just serve them, but to represent Jesus Christ with all my heart while serving them. The Bible says, "…. Thou shalt love thy neighbor as thyself. There is no commandment greater than these" (Mark 12:31). God's grace was the force that allowed me to love and serve more. Considering the abuse I suffered, it would be impossible for me to have a servant's heart without first having faith in Jesus Christ.

God the Holy Spirit was my teacher who instructed me to focus on the needs of others. Through divine instruction, God the Holy Spirit taught me how to think biblically, to live as a Christian, and carry out actions that honor Jesus Christ. I lived from a heart changed by love. When God poured out His love into my heart, it became my responsibility to pour out His love into the hearts of others. Therefore, during my abuse, I could not be disrespectful toward by parents. I had to follow the instructions of God's Word which says, "Love is patient, love is kind. It does not envy, it does not boast, it is not proud. It does not dishonor others, it is not self-seeking, it is not easily angered, it keeps no record of wrongs. Love does not delight in evil but rejoices with the truth. It always protects, always trusts, always hopes, always perseveres" (1 Corinthians 13:4-7).

Kindness, gentleness, patience, and love are the fruits of a servant's heart. I could have embraced hatred, resentment, rebellion, disobeyed my parents when given instructions or refused to do what was asked all together. This type of behavior was not of

God. It would not portray a servant's heart. A Christian should avoid doing wrong or to harm anyone. The Christian must be just, considerate, and speak God's truth with gentleness. In all things I had to represent Jesus Christ. Especially when serving others. The Bible says, "Whatever you do, work at it with all your heart, as working for the Lord…" (Colossians 3:23).

No matter how large or small the task at my home, I was to do them in honor of Jesus Christ. When a task arose, I did not focus on the amount of work it required, my parent's actions, or how I felt. Instead, I focused on doing the task, doing it right, and thanking God for giving me the ability to complete the task. Be it cooking, assisting family members, cleaning, (or whatever the task may be) I believed serving my mother, father, and aunt in my adolescence and young adulthood pleased God. Consequently, I strived to be a humble servant before God. I believed serving others is what pleased God and I made serving God a focal point in my life. I didn't understand why God gave me a heart to serve, but I served my family with the best of my ability. The love I shared with my family was not of my own volition but was from the power of God the Holy Spirit. The Bible teaches that my human nature is selfish, but my new nature is selfless; therefore, I chose to live and walk in my second birth – my new nature.

Doing God's work by serving does not have to be something spectacular. Serving can be giving someone a cup of water. The Bible says, "And if anyone gives even a cup of cold water to one of these little ones who is my disciple, truly I tell you, that person will certainly not lose their reward" (Matthew 10:42). When a believer serves others, they are also serving Almighty God. Serving can be something as simple as being present with someone when they are hurting without saying a word. Serving is saying hello to a stranger with just a smile. Central to a servant's heart is love, which is the essence of God. A servant's heart is the result of being changed by God. The Bible says, "For we are God's handiwork, created in Christ Jesus to do good works..." (Ephesians 2:10). God directs the believer to do good works and serve others. A pleasant feeling of joy always rises within the souls of the believers when they perform tasks in the name of the Lord and Savior Jesus Christ. Serving others aids the believer to become more like Him.

Through Jesus Christ the servant's heart comforts those being served and comforts the servant while changing the servant from the inside out. The servant experiences increased faith and healing for the fatigued soul. My job as the caregiver for my family members was a necessary transition for me because of God's intentions for my life. Serving was part of my healing process and acted to diminish *soul pain*. It produced in me a heart like Jesus Christ; a servant's heart – determined, loving, and peaceful. A servant's heart is a humbled heart, free of pride and arrogance. A servant's heart is also a grateful heart. I am grateful to have the opportunity to receive and carry out tasks ordained by God. I am grateful to have the ability to walk in my salvation with a servant's heart while doing good works for Jesus Christ.

A Willing Vessel

I wondered why Jesus Christ allowed me to endure such horrible abuse that caused such a distressing phenomenon called *soul pain*. *Soul pain* affected my mind, heart, body, and soul. At times, I felt like a sufferer with no hope, nowhere to turn, and no one to confide in. *Soul pain* was a like a roaring lion within my soul causing an eruption of spiritual warfare. Spiritual warfare was foreign to me and I did not understand its impact. For this reason, I suffered *soul pain* in silence. It was obvious that depravity and the enemy's presence was all around me. Satan had control of my parents and a foothold in my family structure for years. As I got older, I believed Jesus Christ was always with me, would not forsake me, and suffering was part of God's plan.

Through faith in Jesus Christ, I chose not to dwell on my abuse, dishonor God, dishonor my grandmother, my parents, or myself. The Bible says, "Therefore, if anyone cleanses himself from what is dishonorable, he will be a vessel for honorable use…" (2 Timothy 2:21). As my faith grew, I believed God's Word was true and I had to live as if my life depended on it. I had to believe that Jesus Christ loved and would deliver me from *soul pain*. He was my hope and my refuge.

For a while, the mirror was my enemy. The reflected image revealed the turmoil Satan caused deep in my soul, confusion in my mind, and pain in my heart. I could not see the wonderful human being that God created in my reflection. There were two battles playing out in my spiritual life at the same time. One battle that was waged externally by my parents caused horrific abuse.

The other battle was waged internally between sin and righteousness, both battles causing *soul pain*. The Bible says, "And lead us not into temptation, but deliver us from the evil one" (Matthew 6:13). God the Holy Spirit gave me the power to resist acts of sin and humbled my heart to become a servant of Almighty God. God gives gifts of forgiveness, grace, mercy, and love to believers to be the example of Jesus Christ in this world. Life can be difficult and unfair but it is essential that we hold onto God's unchanging hand and relying on all the gifts from God in order to serve and love others as Jesus Christ does.

God will always be first in my life. God the Holy Spirit taught me to represent Jesus Christ and to care for my family through abuse. I was given a humbled heart for service and grace to love my enemies. My good work of service was not done as a display of how good I was, but done to display Jesus Christ that dwells within me. Humble acts of service I performed were for the eyes of Jesus Christ to see and not for me to boast. It was a blessing to know that I had a Heavenly Father. It was a blessing that God gave me tasks to accomplish. God the Holy Spirit dwells in my heart and continually changes me into a humble, loving serving Christian.

I was remarkably created to be a vessel made in God's image. I am to serve Him and do good works for Him. The Bible says, "Know that the LORD has set apart his faithful servant for himself..." (Psalm 4:3). I am set apart as a precious jewel of Almighty God, and Jesus Christ, the King of Kings. I am blessed to enjoy the abundant life Jesus Christ promised. I have clarity of mind manifested by God the Holy Spirit, while I have a mind to think with Jesus Christ, to dwell on divine things and not things of the world. Through all the negative effects from *soul pain* I sustained as a young child, I am so thankful that I desired to become a *willing vessel* to please God, to be used by Him, and be a representative of His Son, Jesus Christ. I am so thankful that my God will never leave me nor forsake me.

The Transforming Power

of God's Grace

Chapter 11

Life Can Be Bitter and Sweet

". . . I have come that they may have life and

have it abundantly". (John 10:10)

ॐ ॐ ॐ ॐ ॐ ॐ

Spiritual bankruptcy was common in my family and as a result my childhood and early adolescent years were very bitter. A cloud of evil hovered over the souls of my parents for many seasons. Heinous acts of abuse committed by my parents resulted in overwhelming suffering. If such acts were exposed, it would have brought shame upon my family. However, something else happened during those times as well. My sweet grandmother made me memorize Psalm 23 so that I could pray the Psalm each night before I went to sleep. I did not understand its meaning then, but oh how it has touched my soul through the years – even today.

The Lord is my shepherd; I shall not want. He maketh me to lie down in green pastures: he leadeth me beside the still waters. He restoreth my soul: he leadeth me in the paths of righteousness for his name's sake. Yea, though I walk through the valley of the shadow of death, I will fear no evil: for thou art with me; thy rod and thy staff they comfort me. Thou preparest a table before me in the presence of mine enemies: thou anoinest my head with oil; my cup runneth over. Surely goodness and mercy shall follow me all the days of my life: and I will dwell in the house of the Lord forever. (Psalm 23:1-6)

Almighty God was my caring Heavenly Father who kept me with a sound mind. Jesus Christ kept His promise to be my deliverer, redeemer, and savior. God the Holy Spirit ministered to my broken heart through years of abuse and shared with me the truth of God's Word as it applied to my life. God the Holy Spirit was instrumental, keeping me confident in seeking the correct perspective of life, spirituality, and divine healing for my soul, making it possible for me to see how the words of Psalm 23 have been interwoven into many aspects of my life, past and present. I needed this calming Psalm to nourish my heavy-laden soul. In fact, God used this Psalm to keep me steadfast and able to see His presence through my *soul pain*. Yes, *soul pain* was part of my life, but I chose not to feel sorry for myself. I chose to be led by God the Holy Spirit and do what was right before God.

Yea Though I walk through the valley of the shadow of death, I will fear no evil: for though art with me; thy rod and thy staff they comfort me.

Satan stole the loving parental relationships in my life. I walked through the valley of the shadow of death for a long while, but it was there, I spiritually grew and finally understood what God the Holy Spirit meant by telling me "do not take on my parents' sins." Christians know that sin is an affront before God because of His holiness. When God the Holy Spirit admonished

Freedom From Soul PainLife Can Be Bitter and Sweet

me not to "take on my parents' sins," it meant, my sins are my sins and I am accountable for what I do, not what others do. I was not accountable for the sins of my parents. I had to let God deal with their sins, their actions, and I had to concentrate on not sinning myself. To do that, I had to focus on things above in heaven and not on the actions of others. This meant that though my parents weren't the typical loving parents, I still had to respect and obey them because it was what God expected of me, after all, they gave me life.

While *soul pain* reigned in my life, I resided in the loving arms of Jesus Christ to persevere in my darkest hours. Prayer was a constant for me. God foreknew what would take place in my life. He foreknew I would need comfort, and spiritual care. The Bible says, "…according to the foreknowledge of God the Father, through the sanctifying work of the Spirit, to be obedient to Jesus Christ and sprinkled with his blood: Grace and peace be yours in abundance" (1 Peter 1:2). God knew I needed Jesus Christ in my life at an early age to keep me grounded, humbled, and focused. In this way, the Godhead was alive and active in my life even though I was too young to realize it.

In the valley of the shadow of death, God gave me the task to take care for my family and I had to become as wise as an adult in my youth. Satan wanted to take my focus off God, but I had to carry out the tasks given to me by yielding to God's Word through suffering. As an only child, I had to grow up quickly and manage our household. For example, the store around the corner from our house allowed my father to purchase food and household products on a weekly tab. I purchased deli foods, can goods, pasta products, and snacks. The products were unhealthy. Too much salt, fat, and sugar, but we were blessed because we were able to eat.

Part Two — The Transforming Power of God's Grace

Our home had a coal-fired furnace in the basement with radiators in each room. In the winter, it was my responsibility to make sure the house was kept warm. I strained to lift heavy shovels of coal into the furnace on winter mornings. This was a back breaking chore I hated. My mother and aunt were unable to shovel the coal and most of the time my father was not at home to do it. I taught myself how to bleed the radiators in the house to release air that built up over the summer and fill them with the required amount of water. This had to be done every year before winter arrived to allow the radiators to work properly throughout the cold season. On cold mornings, I was the first person up to poke the fire in the furnace, igniting the smoldering coals, and putting extra coal into the furnace. As the water circulated, I remember hearing loud banging noises in the radiators as heat began to rise throughout the house. When my family began to move around in the morning the house would be nice and warm. To make sure the house was warm all through the day, I would put extra shovels of coal on the fire so that the fire would not burn out before I returned home from school.

Thou preparest a table before me in the presence of mine enemies: thou anointest my head with oil; my cup runneth over.

For a season, my parents were my enemies. My parents were alcoholics and alcohol addiction is a disease that can make a person do horrible things that a rational person would never do. Performing atrocious acts in a drunken stupor, denying the acts ever happened, or being oblivious to inflicted harm does not negate personal responsibility or accountability. My parents had a lot to answer for. Unfortunately, restoration and reconciliation of the parent-child relationship never materialized. There was no dialogue or apology regarding the abuse. Instead, the abuse was never addressed. The offending parties never asked for forgiveness, but I forgave because, as a Christian, that was what I was supposed to do. It is also amazing that Jesus Christ's power can even change the heart of the believer's enemies. Further, I refused to potentially continue the generational curse of alcoholism, physical abuse, sexual perversion, and personal dysfunction prevalent within my family all because I refused to forgive.

The last time my father took me to his janitor's office (the place where he molested me on many occasions), anxiety began to rise again in my soul. My father unlocked and opened the office door, paused, turned, and looked down at me with the strangest look on his face. Without a word, he shut the door, we did not enter the office, we left the building. I don't know what went through my father's mind at the time, but the sexual abuse I endured at the hands of my father finally ended. The season for all the physical, sexual, mental, and emotional abuse ceased. I was thirteen years old. This was another turning point in my life. Without expressing my feelings to anyone, *soul pain* began to diminish. When I became a teenager, Jesus Christ gave me divine healing for my *soul pain*. I thanked God for answering my years of desperate and heavy-hearted prayers. After my abuse ended, there was a different presence in my home and finally the tumultuous interactions among family members in the household ended.

My relationship with my parents remained unemotional and uneventful. There were no hugs or heart-to-heart talks. A loving and trusting family relationship was an illusion. My childhood was a mixture of true love from my grandmother, warped love from my parents, and muted childhood secrets. My life evolved from disorder to dependency and caregiving. Unfortunately, a healthy, and wholesome union within my family never materialized. Instead, I developed a guarded relationship with my father and a supportive relationship with my mother.

I recall my father telling my mother on numerous occasions that he would not live to reach the age of 40 years old. I never understood why he thought that way. My mother would tell him that he was crazy and to be quiet. No one I knew talked about their death so casually. My father coughed a lot but refused to go to a doctor. One summer evening, the police came to our home to tell my mother and I that my father had died. He died on March 4, 1974. He was 39 years old. He died of pneumonia, while he slept in the bed I would sleep in when I visited my grandparent's home. For a while I wondered if God took my father's life at an early age because of the molestation. I will never know, but I know he was judged by God. Everyone has to give a personal account of their life before a Mighty God. God's grace enabled me to forgive the hurt. Healing and wholeness are free gifts from God that I accepted. My healing process began with God the Holy Spirit and God's Word.

Through it all, I chose to praise God for keeping me alive. I was given a grateful heart to know Almighty God was in my life. For a time, I feared my parents, but knowing Jesus Christ made the difference in how I handled my abuse in the valley of death. God the Holy Spirit gave me the power of grace to love my enemies when the world said I shouldn't. The evil that was in my life was replaced with God's promised comfort and peace. God's transforming love gave me a new spirit and new life in the place where *soul pain* once haunted me.

My way of thinking was faith in Jesus Christ and my faith kept me going. I remembered what my grandmother taught me. The Bible says. "Now faith is confidence in what we hope for and assurance about what we do not see" (Hebrews 11:1). Humbly, I tried to make my faith the starting and ending point of how I thought. Faith to me was and is believing God is in control of everything seen and unseen. Faith to me was and is believing that the Holy Scriptures are the absolute truth of all things. Faith to me is the evidence that Jesus Christ died on the cross for every life past, present, and future. Faith to me is believing no matter what happens in the natural world, God has already resolved the issues in heaven.

God prepared a magnificent meal for a very special guest – His child. I am humbly thankful that He prepares, serves, and gives wisdom to those who love His Son, Jesus Christ. His child's enemies maybe near the table but are not permitted to partake in the celebration. They are only able to look at how wonderfully God loves, embraces, and cherishes His children. Anointing the head with oil was a common practice with the Jews in antiquity. It signified a confirmation of an official position. Anointing the believer with God the Holy Spirit gives God's children official position in the family of Jesus Christ. Blessings overflow from those who have faith in Jesus Christ. God can do far more abundantly than what His child can ever ask or think. My distressed heart was ultimately soothed by the Lord and Savior Jesus Christ. The Godhead was the power and presence that dwelt and moved in my life. The Godhead was available to heal the *soul pain.*

He maketh me to lie down in green pastures: he leadeth me beside the still waters.

God gives believers sustenance for the body, mind, and soul. Believers are also given family, friends, and agape love. Most believers have busy lives, but God wants believers to take time to rest. While resting, the mind is refreshed, hearts can find contentment, bodies are reenergized, and souls rest in the comfort of God's love. Almighty God allows His children to lie down in the green pasture of God's Word, covenants, and promises. The green pasture is where the believer finds ultimate rest. The green pasture is where God's Word can be consistently grazed upon and *soul pain* can be dismantled.

Life can be a difficult road to travel, but the choice to please God makes life worthwhile. If allowed, Psalm 23 can become calming words for the hurting soul. There is a transformation that takes place in the crevices of the dark dead soul when God the Holy Spirit is allowed to search the weary soul for things that are ungodly and things that turn the believer away from Almighty God. There is an astounding feeling of freedom deep in the soul when God's Words stirs the spirit and opens the spiritual heart, mind, ears, eyes. With Jesus Christ, a life that was once bitter can be transformed into a life that becomes sweet, loving, kind, and victorious.

Chapter 12

All About Me

"For the desires of the flesh are against the Spirit, and the desires of the Spirit are against the flesh, for these are opposed to each other, to keep you from doing the things you want to do".

(Galatians 5:17)

જે જે જે જે જે જે

Moving from adolescence into young adulthood, *soul pain* did not have the same effect as it did when I was young. In 1973, a year after high school, I worked at North Charles General Hospital as a Laboratory Aide. I remained there for 13 years. As I matured into adulthood, the memories of how God the Holy Spirit healed my *soul pain* faded. I failed to recall the way God the Holy Spirit conquered the turmoil and dysfunction in my family. I lost my way. I chose to live for me. To paraphrase Revelation 2:4, I chose to forsake the love I had at first. I knew what Jesus Christ required of me, but as a young adult, I wanted to live life my way. Sadly, I failed to recall the divine healing of my *soul pain.* Instead, I allowed my youth and spiritual immaturity to dictate my choices. I chose to enjoy the world. I was not mindful of what God the Holy Spirit had done to heal my *soul pain*. My humanity was weak.

Being spiritually immature, I did not always acknowledge Jesus Christ's presence in my life. I looked forward to going to the disco on the weekends with my girlfriends. We would hit the floor and dance the night away. I allowed the distractions and busyness of my day to keep me from going to church, faithfully reading God's Word, spending quiet time with the Lord, and spending time in the assembly of believers. It was easy to find something else to do instead of devotion. I was not a member of a church family to help me grow in the faith. I was too busy doing the things that made me happy. However, I would always pray to God at night.

Being me focused, my primary aim was what I wanted in life. I felt invincible. I was an independent young woman. I was my own person. I wanted to look good, feel great, and live life my way. My life was all about me and I chose to live it on the fence. I became like a pendulum – swinging back and forth between the divine and the carnal. I failed to remember my dual citizenship. My physical birth gives me US citizenship but my second birth through Jesus Christ gives me citizenship in heaven. I was not living as a citizen of heaven nor was I bearing good fruit. My tree became bare. I thought I could have the best of both worlds, the kingdom of this world and the kingdom of heaven. The Bible says, "… forget not all his benefits" (Psalm 103:2). I failed to consider how God the Holy Spirit intervened to help me out of the snares of *soul pain*. I ignored how Almighty God blessed me. Therefore, my early adulthood was a time of living from the flesh. I pompously lived independently and with prideful self-awareness. Not guarding my heart or choosing wisely what I watched with my eyes or heard with my ears.

I walked around for years juggling my life between living as a Carnal Christian and living as a Devout Christian – between being self-righteous and being sincerely righteous. I lived the life I thought was right as a Christian without understanding the magnitude of being completely surrendered to the Lord Jesus Christ. I knew who Jesus Christ was from a young age, but I was not yet willing to totally submit and commit my life to Him. I thank God that He continually granted mercy on me by allowing His angles to protect me from harm I might inflict on myself or harm I might inflict on others. I arrogantly expected Jesus Christ to accept what I thought was right as being a Christian. With spiritual haughtiness, I thought I was not a sinful person. I thought I was good enough to get into heaven the way I was. In my eyes, there was nothing wrong with me. I didn't need to change. I knew who Jesus Christ was and I had a relationship with Him. What else did I need? It was the people that did not accept Jesus Christ as their Lord and Savior and backsliders that refused to change their sinful ways who were the ones that weren't getting into heaven. The nourishment that was so desperately needed from Psalm 23 was silent during this time of my life. Regrettable on many occasions during my young adult life, I was not receptive to Jesus Christ's teachings. Selfishly I took Almighty God, Jesus Christ, and God the Holy Spirit for granted and endeavored to enjoy both worlds: the divine and the natural.

There were many circumstances in my young adult life that turned me away from God and eventually back to God. It is with perseverance that God the Holy Spirit gave me strength not to succumb to the many failings young adults encounter. As I grew in understanding of God's truth, a desire to obey Almighty God once again became central in my life. My life changed from an *all about me* attitude to all about Jesus Christ. The story of the gospel was real once more. God's love overwhelmed me once again and He won over my heart for good. The Bible says, "Consider it pure joy, my brothers and sisters, whenever you face trials of many kinds, because you know that the testing of your faith produces perseverance" (James1:2-3).

Thankfully, I did not remain ignorant, I understood I needed God the Holy Spirit for direction in life. My childish days were over. I was a guilty sinner, and I was no different than the worst sinner on earth, I needed a Savior. I am acceptable before God because of what Jesus Christ did for me and not because of anything I did. Even though my *soul pain* had diminished, it was not forgotten. S*oul pain* did not crush me, it made me stronger. I was able to rededicate my mind, heart, and soul to the Lord. My life could not remain all about me, but became about worshipping, honoring, and glorifying God always. Jesus Christ is the sustainer of my life and He continues to bless me.

Chapter 13

Return to My First Love

"And he died for all, that those who live should no longer live for themselves but for him who died for them and was raised again".

(2 Corinthians 5:15)

ৡৡৡৡৡৡ

I finally understood what God the Holy Spirit meant when He told me, "I will make your enemies your footstool." Those were words played over and over in my mind for many years. My father died at an early age and my mother became helpless, humbled, and frail after the car accident. She needed me to assist her with her daily needs and I did not mind one bit. I thanked God for whatever task He placed before me on my life's journey. The difficult things I encountered in life drew me closer to Him. I was blessed with the saving knowledge of Jesus Christ's continual and abundant love. I had an awakening of my faith and Psalm 23 once more became beautiful music within my soul.

"The Lord is my shepherd; I shall not want."

I met my husband in 1983 and we married in 1987. I was drawn to my husband because of his intelligence. I observed him to be a good father, and a genuinely nice person. However, dating him put me in contradiction with God's word because he was an unbeliever. 2 Corinthians 6:14 says, "Do not be yoked together with unbelievers. For what do righteousness and wickedness have in common? Or what fellowship can light have with darkness?"

I was tested on many occasions during the marriage. I remember being admitted into the hospital for testing because I was diagnosed with mitral valve prolapse. Feeling very weak and afraid, I prayed to God for healing that night in the hospital. I prayed to God by saying, "God I am in the hospital lying flat on my back and I can do nothing. Please heal me." God the Holy Spirit responded by saying, "I know, I put you there". I was shocked and stunned by the response. Again, I wondered if God was speaking to me or if I was imaging it. I was ill, but I was also being chastised by God? Yes, and God showed me why. God revealed that I was a "spiritually self-righteous person," and he used my husband to reveal it. I believe the chastisement I received in the hospital happened because I was not living in God's will.

In my mind, I was spiritually superior to my husband. I thought my husband was weak in his faith and I was stronger in mine. My husband professed his Jewish faith, but he did not practice nor know much about Judaism. I knew more about Judaism then he did and; therefore, I felt superior in my faith. I cried that night in the hospital. I was embarrassed and heartbroken because God showed me that I was a "self-righteous sinner." I stayed in the hospital for a few days for additional testing. While there, I reflected on my faith, behavior, and my relationship with God. After I left the hospital, I purchased a "thank you card" for my husband thanking him for our marriage and I asked for forgiveness. My husband was bewildered and did not understand what the card meant, but I had to make my life right before God. God will take the most difficult circumstances to make Himself known and put His children back on the right path. Again, God made Himself known to me that night when He spoke to me at the hospital.

It was God the Holy Spirit that humbled and convicted me of my sins. Jesus Christ is my true source of goodness, righteousness, and eternal life. A righteous and divine life was set before me and I am a living testimony for God. Although I did not focus on the presence of God the Holy Spirit for a season, He was always with me. The Bible says, "I will instruct you and teach you in the way you should go; I will counsel you with my eye upon you" (Psalm 32:8). After chastisement from Almighty God, I continued praying daily for God the Holy Spirit to teach me to understand God's Word, to gain spiritual wisdom, and understanding. It's important for me to walk by the Spirit and not by sight.

God created marriage and it brings about many opportunities for two people to become one. My husband's family lived in the suburbs with manicured lawns and beautiful detached homes. I came from a dysfunctional family of alcoholics that lived in a poor inner-city neighborhood. Prior to our marriage, a family member of my husband asked him if he thought I was a suitable wife for him because of my upbringing. My husband assured them all that I was the right one. However, while we were dating, I did not address my fiancé's brokenness, hurt, and pain. You see, no matter what family you come from, many have some type of dysfunction.

My husband was a broken spiritual vessel. This became evident early in our marriage as I endured his constant verbal abuse. His first marriage ended in divorce and it took a toll on him mentally and spiritually. However, I will not be a participant in gossiping on what may or may not have happened in his first marriage because I don't know the intimate details of their relationship. The Bible says, "Keep your tongue from evil and your lips from speaking deceit" (Psalm 34:13). I do believe God's heart breaks when a divorce occurs because marriage is a gift and God knows the heartache divorce can cause His children. Sadly, because of divorce, prospective divorcees, and divorced persons can spiral into the darkness of *soul pain*. The Bible says, "For the LORD God of Israel says That He hates divorce…." (Malachi 2:16). There is ample information regarding the trials divorced couples endure. Both parties as well as their children suffer deeply from negative lingering effects of divorce. If not properly resolved, those negative effects can also gravely impact future mates.

It is imperative to make godly choices when selecting a mate. When two people come together to profess their love for each other, each person brings different backgrounds, behaviors, beliefs, and personality traits into the marriage. As time goes on, a couple should grow together as one. This oneness means there may be a cross that one mate brings into the marriage that the other must be willing to bear. This is why believers are admonished to be cautious when they choose a mate. According to 1 Corinthians 7:13-14, ". . . if a woman has a husband who is not a believer and he is willing to live with her, she must not divorce him. For the unbelieving husband has been sanctified through his wife, and the unbelieving wife has been sanctified through her believing husband . . ." In other words, God will bless the unbelieving spouse through the believing spouse, but there is a process associated with acquiring that blessing.

Praise God for those couples that have peace in the home, respect, and love each other. Their relationship sets a good example before their children to become well balanced in life. However, marriages that have strife, marital issues, or *soul pain* should seek Jesus Christ for His divine healing. If one partner is unwilling to do so, it leaves the marriage in limbo and additional strain on the believing partner. I found myself continually praying for my husband and asked God to change his heart. The Bible says, "I will give you a new heart and put a new spirit in you; I will remove from you your heart of stone and give you a heart of flesh" (Ezekiel 36:26).

My marriage was not in a good place for many years and once again I had to deal with *soul pain*. The verbal abuse projected toward me by my husband and the pain of those harsh words caused invisible scars on my heart. My husband's unresolved pain produced anger issues within him. He was dealing with his own *soul pain*. The condition of his heart was broken and deeply crushed. For many years, my husband could not love me as God required of a husband. However, I continued to love and care for him as required of a Christian wife. I lived in a low-level of sadness for almost twenty years. I was asked on several occasions why I stayed in such an abusive relationship. Divorce was not an option for me. I was determined not to pass on a cycle of *soul pain* as a generational curse onto the souls of our children. I desired for my children to choose life and blessing rather than heartache and spiritual death. I turned my marriage over to Jesus Christ. The Bible says, "He (the Lord) heals the brokenhearted and binds up their wounds." (Psalm 147:3). I focused on what God had given our family and not what we did not have. I had a husband, home, and wonderful children. Blessings can be found in chaos if you look hard enough. God is the only one that satisfies completely. I believed Jesus Christ wanted me to be still, to wait to see His glory in my marriage and my life.

One place my husband often found solace was in the presence of his children. My husband looked forward to visitations with his children and yearned to spend time with them. My husband has three lovely children from his previous marriage. They were always respectful and kind toward me, and they still are today. I try to be a good role model for them by loving and caring for them as my own. For many years, my husband dealt with guilt from being separated from his children. Sadly, there is always collateral damage from divorce. Couples should seriously think what's best for the marriage and the long-term effects of divorce on their children. Thankfully, there was no feeling of animosity between my husband's ex-wife and myself or feelings of strife. The Bible says, "A good man brings good things out of the good stored up in his heart…" (Luke 6:45). By the world's standard, exes are more likely to be hostile toward each other in many circumstances. By God's grace, these preconceptions are completely false. When God the Holy Spirit guides your life, it is easy to love and to be courteous. Because of God's grace I have a good relationship with my husband's ex-spouse and his children. As my husband witnessed this in me, it built in him an ability to trust me unconditionally.

In 1988, I had a miscarriage early in my first trimester. After an examination by the doctor and a few tests, I was informed that I lost that pregnancy. I was sad, but I was able to cope with the loss because it was very early in my pregnancy. My Shepard, Jesus Christ, tenderly cared for me and in 1989, I gave birth to our daughter. Her birth was a pivotal moment that changed my life forever as I once again fully committed my life to Jesus Christ. In 1992, I had another miscarriage, and I experienced the same loss in the first trimester. In 1993, I gave birth to our son. I knew I could not give my children material wealth, but I could give them a foundation of faith. I wanted to be a godly example for my children and teach them about God and that He sees and hears everything they think, say, or do. I taught them to develop their own relationship with God through Jesus Christ. I instilled godly values and taught them how to be kind. I also instructed them to treat people with respect, and to love themselves. I told them the importance of praying about everything and putting Jesus Christ first in their lives. I warned them that it may be hard to pray about everything that happens in their lives, but prayer is what God expects them to do.

When I think about teaching moments with my children, I always gave my children two scenarios when making decisions in life. They were to think about: 1) the world's response to an issue; and 2) God's response to that same issue. I would tell them to choose which scenario they thought was correct. When our daughter was 12-years-old, a Y Magazine came to the house. I canceled the subscription, but magazines continued coming in the mail. Flipping through the magazine to the editorial section, there were questions that affected a teen's life (dating, pregnancy, and other matters). I did not like the editor's responses to questions asked by their young teenage customers. I used the questions as teaching moments with my daughter.

We discussed the questions and answers in the magazine. My responses to the questions were from a spiritual point of view and the editor's responses were from a world's viewpoint. After our discussion about the questions, I talked to my daughter about God, life, and family. I prayed that the conversations we had would positively impact her life. Our daughter was blessed to attend a very good private school and graduate from an ivy league college.

Before my son was school age, while the family was sleep, my son and I would go into the kitchen and eat warm deep-dish apple pie with ice cream. Those were special moments that were only between my son and me. We would talk about God and about life. Our son was blessed to attend a very good private school and graduate from a very good University. The Bible says, "Praise the LORD. Blessed are those who fear the LORD, who ind great delight in his commands. Their children will be mighty in the land; the generation of the upright will be blessed" (Psalm 112:1-2).

Marriage is a sacred institution created by God, but for many it comes with undisputable problems and some unresolved issues. One day after one of our many arguments, my husband called to tell me he wanted to talk to me about an issue that was bother-ing him. We went for a drive to a nearby park to talk. During the conversation, I was given an ultimatum by my husband to choose him or Jesus Christ. According to him I couldn't have both. With-out hesitation, I told my husband to prepare the divorce papers because I was not giving up Jesus Christ for him. I was so hurt that night because after all of the work I put into preserving my marriage, I was de initely getting a divorce. The next morning, I did not talk to my husband. He asked what was wrong with me and I reminded him of our conversation the day before. He was lippant and said that he did not mean what he said. I told him to never give me that type of ultimatum ever again. God can use people, objects, and nature to test and grow your faith. This conversation was never mentioned again. I wondered if God used that conversation to test my faith or to challenge his.

For years my husband was unhappy with himself. I suggested we go to marriage counseling and he flatly refused. He said that the counselors had their own problems, and they could not tell him what he needed to do in our marriage. There were many times I wanted out of the marriage, but I wanted my children to be in a home with both a mother and father, while they were growing up. No matter what my husband and I went through, I did not allow our children to disrespect their father nor did I discuss our marital issues with them. Beyond that, I wouldn't leave because I was concerned about who would be watching my children and where they would be staying if I left my husband.

After I dropped my children off at school in the morning, on the way back home or on the way to the office, I would pull the car over and pray for my husband and our marriage. The place where I stopped became a favorite spot for me. It was on a tree lined street with beautiful homes. I prayed at the same spot for several years. My focus was to see how God would end this miserable marriage, so I remained. By 2010, our son was in the 11th grade and I'd had enough of the verbal abuse. I decided when my son left for college, I would leave the marriage. Until that time came, I continued to pray to God to ease my pain and bring peace to the marriage. I prayed these words, "God if you want me to stay in this marriage, please do something, if not, I will leave my husband when our son goes away to college".

As a last-ditch effort, I once again suggested we go to marriage counseling. To my surprise my husband told me to select the counselor. I prayed about what counselor to select. I did not select a female or Christian marriage counselor because I knew there would be push back from my husband. I chose a male Jewish marriage counselor. We were scheduled for weekly counseling sessions for six months. After three counseling sessions, my husband began to change. Our marriage gradually moved from episodes of verbal attacks and mistrust to loving each other with all of our hearts. We did not return to counseling after the third session. Our marriage took a 180-degree turn. I am certain with all my heart that God intervened.

Through prayer I could see the love of God changing my heart and my husband's heart. My husband began to say grace over his food, openly talk about God, and show me true affection. I could see God transforming my husband into as a different man. His transformation made our marriage better. I receive heartfelt love from my husband daily and I have heartfelt love for him. My life has been very bitter, but now it has become very sweet. Even though we celebrated 33 years of marriage in 2020, I continue to pray for my husband and our marriage. I pray because I know who is keeping us. Jesus Christ protects me from evil. He gives me all that I need in this life and the next. He has given me a husband and two beautiful children who love me. Satan stole the loving parental relationship in my youth. He tried to steal the love and joy of my marriage and family in my adulthood, but Almighty God has kept my marriage firmly in a place of restoration. . God has blessed our marriage, our family and our business. I once wondered how God would end my miserable marriage, but I'm so blessed that He intervened. Not only was our marriage revived, but it has thrived.

I worked with my husband in his general contracting business as his office manager for over 30 years. Several people asked my husband how he could live, work, and be with his wife 24 hours a day. His response was, "I can trust her, its other people that I can't trust, and she guards the money." We are still operating our construction business today. Our business was not always great for us, but God allowed the business to turn around for the better.

In the beginning of the business, we started performing home improvement projects. Initially, my husband was too friendly with the employees. He picked them up in the morning, bought them breakfast and lunch, then took them home in the evening after work. Their workmanship was very poor, and the jobs had to be performed twice to get it right.

Through trial and error, we overcame our in-house issues and our company became a certified MBE contractor to do work with Baltimore City and the State of Maryland. Working with the Baltimore City Single Family Housing Program, our company was able to procure five (5) home improvement contracts out of the eight (8) on their weekly list. Interviewing clients in a professional manner gave our company an advantage over the other contractors seeking contracts. The business was doing well for a while until our checks began to be delayed, which made it difficult to pay our business expenses and subcontractors. I was so frustrated because of the lack of revenue, it brought me to tears. There were many times the gas and electric were turned off and we had to stay in hotels. There were times we did not have enough money to buy food. I called myself the Oodles of Noodles Queen. I learned how to cook Raman noodles in many different ways for the family. During the difficult time, my husband found out that a governmental official had our checks diverted from being mailed directly to our office to being mailed to his office. He deliberately withheld our payment checks so that we could not pay our expenses. The official's actions almost put us out of business. After the governmental official's superior found out what he had done, he was made to resign. We were given all the checks that were in the drawer and from that point, all future checks were mailed directedly to our office.

Moving forward, the company expanded from residential construction to commercial construction. We completed several commercial contracts: medical clinics, transportation facilities, and churches. Sadly, a couple of our church clients never paid us for services performed. Combined, the churches owed our company $220,000. We never recouped the cost incurred on these projects. We never sued the churches, but praise God, whenever one door closed, God opens another.

"He restoreth my soul: he leadeth me in the paths of righteousness for his name's sake."

My dark secret stayed with me until I was 47 years old. I revealed my family secret in a pastoral counseling class. The students were asked to share something about themselves that no one knew. I shared a testimony of how I overcame *soul pain* with no condemnation and God's love. There was empathy for me among my classmates. I was able to share my testimony about my past for the first time with others without difficulty. I shared my testimony of how the Godhead healed my *soul pain*. I felt free. I also shared my testimony with a classmate, while I attended Lancaster Bible College years later. My classmate suggested that I share my life's experience with others. My classmate ministers to women who were incarcerated, and she has seen a lot of broken women. Some of the women have suffered the same *soul pain* I suffered. She is the reason I am sharing my story with others. Hopefully, my testimony will have a positive impact on many, prompting them to turn to God for deliverance while prompting many to turn away the things that prevent them from receiving God's peace.

As I grew older and wiser, I craved God's truths and to be in constant communion with Jesus Christ. I longed to be the person

Jesus Christ wanted me to be. I tried to be sensitive to the leading of God the Holy Spirit. God the Holy Spirit directed me to be established in my thoughts and actions. I thank God He was involved in my life even before I knew and accepted His Son, Jesus Christ as my Lord and Savior. I thank God for the Holy roles of the Godhead. God the Father created me, God the Son saved me, and God the Holy Spirit is continually teaching and guiding me to live as a child of God. It was and is extremely important for the me to acknowledge, embrace, and respect the Father, Son, and Holy Spirit. The Bible says, "This is what we speak, not in words taught us by human wisdom but in words taught by the Spirit, explaining spiritual realities with Spirit-taught words" (1 Corinthians 2:13). The lessons I learned about the Godhead are very valuable. The more I desired to know Jesus Christ; I was never denied His divinity or His power.

Years ago, I remember having a conversation with a sister-in-law about my desire to attend Bible College. Her response was "God will make it happen." When our son entered college, I went back to college. At 57 years of age. I enrolled at Washington Bible College that merged with Lancaster Bible College. I earned a Bachelor of Arts Degree in Biblical Studies. After graduation, I fulfilled another desire by enrolling in the Real Estate Development Master's Program at University of Maryland College Park. I graduated at 61 years of age in 2015. God has blessed me by giving me the desires of my heart. God has blessed me so much and I try to bless others through kindness and being and Ambassador of Jesus Christ. Jesus Christ restored my soul to fullness, and He has led me on a path of forgiveness and kindness. He continues to bless me beyond what I could ever imagine.

God leads His children to the living water that is freely given by His Son, Jesus Christ. Where God leads, I must follow. He restored my soul to usefulness. Usefulness so that God could be glorified. Nothing about the child of God is useless or worthless. God can bring life to things that are withered, shattered, destroyed, and spiritually dead. Jesus came to give life to the dead soul, set the captives free, and to show the world His Father in Heaven.

"Surely goodness and mercy shall follow me all the days of my life."

Through Jesus Christ, I have eternal life now. Jesus Christ came to this world not only to save but be influential in the lives His Father in Heaven sent Him. Every day I see God's goodness and mercy through His love. I see God's goodness and mercy in nature when the sun rises in the morning and when the moon shines at night. I see God's presence in so many parts of my life.

"And I will dwell in the house of the Lord forever."

While I was in college, I was disappointed about the state of my spiritual life because the workloads of school and business were overwhelming. I did not have time for devotion, and I missed being able to spend time with the God, or commune with Jesus Christ as I use to. I prayed to God that when I graduated college, He'd send me to a small Bible believing church. While in school, I tithed to churches in the area where I lived even though I was not a church member. After I graduated, I visited a church in my neighborhood several times until I became a member. It is a true Bible believing church where God's Word is taught and preached consistently. When my mother died, I received several calls of condolences from the pastor, his wife, and church members that I didn't even know. As a new member, I felt that I was part of a church family that cared and not a member in name only.

Throughout my life, God always heard my cries. In the heavenly realm, God quietly orchestrates the affairs of His children, so that the best outcomes for them are seen in the natural realm. He has blessed my life tremendously and I have a wonderful life. I'm glad I chose to keep my mind on the Godhead. I was so dumb to live as a backslider, but when I became a mother, from that point on, I looked to Almighty God for everything. I humbly submitted my soul to Jesus Christ with gratitude. I have pure joy observing how God reveals Himself to me. Best of all, I can dwell in the house of the Lord forever.

Deep down I knew I had to return to my first love. I had to honor God completely. I take delight in praising God every day. I no longer wanted to neglect my faith. My life was not about me, but about worshipping, honoring, and glorifying Almighty God always. Jesus Christ is the sustainer of my life and He continues to bless me. I am grateful that God the Holy Spirit is always with me.

Chapter 14

To Be One With Jesus Christ

"But whoever is united with the Lord is one with him in spirit".

(1 Corinthians 6:17)

৵৵৵৵৵৵৵

As my faith matured in Jesus Christ, I could clearly see the Godhead's presence in my personal and professional life and in the lives of my immediate family. I could also discern the Godhead in the lives of others. In the last chapter, I spoke about my marriage, children, education, and the reason for writing this book. This book has traced a life of horrible trials and tribulations; however, what was written does not equate to an entire life of misery. If my suffering has taught me anything, it is that seasons of misery can turn into a life of many blessings. When Jesus Christ is in the midst of our suffering, we have a protector, comforter, and healer with us. However, we only realize this if we stay focused on Jesus Christ.

The Bible says, "For the LORD God is a sun and shield; the LORD bestows favor and honor; no good thing does he withhold from those whose walk is blameless" (Psalm 84:11). There is nothing God will withhold from His child. God did not promise us monetary wealth, worldly success, or perfect health. What He did promise us was His love, forgiveness, grace, mercy, and His Son Jesus Christ. Through Jesus Christ I was able to overcome the many mental, emotional, and physical scars of *soul pain* and God has brought many of my desires into existence. Feeling sorry for myself was simply out of the question. It would have hindered me from living a life of freedom as I became one with God and, therefore, walked in the appropriate manner before Him.

I had an unpretentious misunderstanding of what it meant to become one with Jesus Christ. With the passage of time, I realized it was a blessing and honor to have Almighty God willing to be one in Spirit with a sinner like me. The Bible says, "...But you were washed, you were sanctified, you were justified in the name of the Lord Jesus Christ and by the Spirit of our God" (1 Corinthians 6:11). Jesus Christ cleansed me spiritually and awakened my dreadful dead soul. I have been purchased by the blood of Jesus Christ. I am His light, eyes, ears, mouth, and feet here on earth. It is God the Holy Spirit who daily unites my soul and spirit through faith in the Lord Jesus Christ, allowing me to be one in the Spirit in Him. Being united with Jesus Christ in one spirit, I must not purposely become an instrument of sin. The Bible says, "...whoever believes in me will do the works I have been doing, and they will do even greater things than these..." (John 14:12). How awesome is it for me to know that I will be able to do great works while I am here on this earth for Jesus Christ? I will be an influencer in the world for the things of God as I worship Jesus Christ and obey His commands.

When I attended a weekly Pastoral Care class at St. Joseph Hospital, I interacted with patients and, at times, the presence of the Lord was evident. I even interacted with patients who were racist towards me because of the color of my skin. Racism is pure sin and nothing else. My duty was to minister Jesus Christ to lost souls. The patient's spiritual state was at stake and that is what I focused on. Jesus Christ was what their dark souls needed more than for me to worry about someone not liking me because of the color of my skin. I prayed with and for each patient no matter who they were. In an encounter with a patient, it was a pleasure to see the change of heart in a racist patient when Jesus Christ was ministered. A smile was on the face of the patient when I left the room. I shared the encounter with my mentor. At first, she was upset because of the offensive statement made, but I told her to focus on how I was able to minister to the patient apart from what was said. We both agreed that to be able to look past the faults of others was an amazing demonstration of the power of God.

Being one with Jesus Christ enables believers to stand before the world as His ambassadors. The Bible says, "We are therefore Christ's ambassadors, as though God were making his appeal through us. We implore you on Christ's behalf: Be reconciled to God" (2 Corinthians 5:20). To be Jesus Christ's ambassadors is to share heaven with the world by serving, caring for, and loving humanity. Ambassadors have infectious spirits. People in the world know that there is something different about Ambassadors of Jesus Christ, but they cannot quite put their finger on it. The infectious spirit is joy in Jesus Christ. God pours His spirit through His ambassadors into others. Jesus Christ's ambassadors are on duty all day, every day; therefore, they must emulate Jesus Christ by being humbled by grace, and living by faith before a just and Holy God. As a result, Jesus Christ and the goodness of heaven can be seen in His ambassadors.

Ultimately, being one with Jesus Christ allows His children to freely approach the throne of grace at any time and any place. The Bible says, "Draw near to God, and he will draw near to you" (James 4:8). Faith in Jesus Christ allows believers to have a new nature, with a new heart, a new home, and become one with Him. To be one with Jesus Christ, believers must glorify the Father always. To be one with Jesus Christ, Jesus Christ and believers live in one spirit. The believer must live holy and boldly with hope for this world, hope in the gospel, and hope in the life that God created for them. The Bible says, "For I am not ashamed of the gospel, because it is the power of God that brings salvation to everyone who believes..." (Romans 1:16). Through faith, life can be lived victoriously. I am a long way from being the person that God wants me to be, but I am not the person that I use to be. Thankfully, I still can be one with Jesus Christ.

Chapter 15

Healed By Grace and Blessed For Obedience

".....proclaiming the good news of the kingdom and healing every disease and sickness among the people". (Matthew 4:23)

కకకకకకక

I have been both a recipient and a witness of God's divine healing. *Soul pain* shattered my innocent soul, but the glory of my Heavenly Father prevailed over my life to mend all of my broken pieces. As a recipient of God's divine healing, God healed my physical body from many medical ailments, and spiritually healed my broken soul. God cradled my shattered soul to a place of comfort and joy in the Lord. Just to mention the name of Jesus Christ brings joy to my spiritual heart and hope to my weak soul. His name is the antidote I need for my exhausted soul. As time passed, I did not feel uncomfortable being a Christian. I did not know or understand all of the statutes, testimonies, and commandments of God, but my soul was healed to the point where

I could reach out to others to tell the redemption story of Jesus Christ. I could tell the world how great Almighty God was and will always be.

God blessed me to be a witness of His divine healing in the life of my cousin whom we will refer to as Jennifer. Friday morning before Easter 1998, Jennifer's sister called me to tell me that Jennifer had been rushed to the hospital in a coma. Doctors shocked the family because they did not expect her to live very long. Jennifer was 39 years old and a mother of one. Months prior, I visited Jennifer regularly at her apartment. While there, I cooked for her, talked about God, or whatever came to mind and helped her prepare her Living Will and guardianship papers. I also accompanied her on many of her doctor's appointments. Jennifer was in pain most of the time and her doctors had difficulty diagnosing what she was suffering from. With sadness, Jennifer would tell me about one of her doctor's visit where she overheard the nurses infer that she was imagining her pain. She knew that something was wrong with her, but she felt no one believed her.

After visiting several doctors, she was finally diagnosed with a very rare form of cancer. She was diagnosed with an aggressive tumor, called *"leiomyosarcoma."* This was a virulent form of cancer that spreads quickly throughout the body. The day before falling into a coma, Jennifer's close girlfriend was visiting her at home. Her friend stated that in the middle of the visit, Jennifer was lying in bed and saw her mother standing in her bedroom doorway with outstretched hands. Jennifer became scared and asked her friend "Do you see my mom in the doorway?" Her friend said, "I don't see anyone in the room." Jennifer's mother died years ago. By the end of the day Jennifer had slipped into a coma and she was rushed to the hospital.

Jennifer's sister called me again and stressed the importance that I visit Jennifer. Several events transpired after the phone call. Friday night while I was sleeping, God the Holy Spirit spoke instructing me to take some anointing oil and anoint Jennifer. I was not sure if God was really speaking to me or if it was my imagination. The next day, I obeyed God the Holy Spirit's instruction and purchased a bottle of olive oil. I poured some of the oil in a plastic bag and prayed over it. After church service that Easter Sunday, my family and I traveled to visit Jennifer at the hospital. When we arrived at the hospital, Jennifer was lying flat on her back on the bed with gauze pads placed over her eyes. She was not receiving any IV fluids or connected to any hospital devices. I was informed by family members that the doctor suggested that the family begin making final arrangements for Jennifer. Hope for her leaving the hospital alive was fading. When my husband took our children to the cafeteria, I asked Jennifer's daughter if I could say a prayer for her mother. She said yes, while praying I anointed Jennifer with oil and said a prayer. I did not pray a long eloquent prayer, I said what was on my heart. It was a heartfelt prayer for healing.

Monday, I received a call from Jennifer's partner. He asked me if I knew where Jennifer's Living Will and guardianship papers were. I explained to him where they were, but he could not find them. I visited them the following day. I went directly to the hospital to visit Jennifer before I went to her apartment. To my surprise Jennifer was awake. She recognized my voice when I entered the room. I heard her say "Thank you God for bringing my cousin here to see me." Tears began to well up in my eyes. I was shocked and happy at the same time to see how quickly she had improved. I don't know why, but during our conversation, I asked Jennifer if she wanted to get married. She said "yes." I called her fiancé while I was at the hospital that evening, and Jenifer sang *"Stand By Your Man"* to Henry over the telephone. When I got to Jennifer's apartment, I asked Jennifer's partner if he would marry her. He said that "he would marry her anytime or anyplace." To the glory of God and the doctors' bewilderment, Jennifer left the hospital, got married, and lived for a short time after her discharge from the hospital. She was able to do something she wanted to do for 15 years, get married.

God is our healer. Jennifer was divinely healed to leave the hospital and marry the love of her life before God took her home to be with Him. God gave Jennifer divine strength in her illness. The Bible says, "The *LORD* sustains them on their sickbed and restores them from their bed of illness" (Psalms 41:3). My heart was so filled with joy because God allowed me to see such an incredible miracle. I was a witness of divine healing. I thought to myself, if I never see another miracle again, I saw one with Jennifer.

In the winter of 2013, from Monday through Wednesday, my husband complained of pain in his stomach. He thought it was indigestion from something he ate. He also complained of pains in his lower extremities, and it was difficult for him to walk. When he felt the pain, he would get on his knees and lean against the sofa or bed. This position gave him a little relief. On Thursday morning of that same week, while my husband was preparing to go to a job site, he told me he felt a sensation of extreme coldness in his chest. He put on a heavier coat and left to go to a job site. He called me from the job site to let me know he was not feeling well. He was having a difficult time walking and decided to go to the hospital. His primary doctor's office was located in the hospital. I suggested instead of going to the emergency room he go directly to his doctor's hospital office. I said a prayer for him after I hung up the phone. My husband was immediately seen at his doctor's office. About an hour later, I received a call from my husband's doctor informing me that my husband had a heart attack. He stated that it was unknown when the heart attack occurred and that my husband was rushed by ambulance to a nearby hospital for a cardiac catheterization procedure.

After the phone call, I contacted the children to let them know about their father then rushed to the hospital. Once the catherization was completed, the family was allowed to enter my husband's room. There was a double monitor in the room displaying my husband's before and after heart images. The before image showed his main aorta was 100% blocked. The after image showed the aorta completely opened. A stent was placed in his heart. The doctor told my husband that he had the "widow maker" and he was one in a million to survive this condition. We were made aware that prior to his surgery, my husband's body developed another way to circulate the blood flow to his lower extremities and back to his heart. My husband was divinely healed by the power of our Heavenly Father and I was able to witness another miraculous healing by Almighty God.

I too was a recipient of God's divine healing when I was diagnosed with thyroid disease. In 2000, I had a sore throat, I noticed a protrusion at the base of my neck, and I was sweating excessively. I made an appointment with my primary physician and she immediately ordered a surgical consultation to determine if my thyroid should be removed. My primary doctor's office manager had thyroid surgery the previous year and was eager to detail her experience with thyroid surgery, the operation process, and answer my questions or concerns. I visited the surgeon and he suggested that I have an ultrasound done to determine the condition of my thyroid. The ultrasound detected a solid mass on one thyroid lobe and several enlarged nodules on the other thyroid lobe. I had a needle aspiration to determine if the thyroid mass and nodules were cancerous or benign. The aspiration was the most painful medical procedure I have ever experienced. The needle aspiration ruled out cancer in both the thyroid mass and the nodules.

I did not feel comfortable being rushed to have surgery. Instead, I elected to have a second opinion and made an appointment with an endocrinologist. While I waited for my appointment date, I periodically placed my hands on my neck and prayed to God for healing. The new endocrinologist ordered another ultrasound to verify the current condition of my thyroid. While lying on the exam table, the ultrasound technician asked me which side were the nodules on? Her question puzzled me a bit. I told her that the nodules were on the right side and a solid mass on the left side. She excused herself and left the room to review my last ultrasound results. When she returned, she told me "someone must really like you because there is no solid mass, and the nodules are reduced." I told her "It wasn't somebody, it was God who looked out for me." I was surprised that the technician spoke to me about my results. From my previous experience working in a hospital, medical techs don't usually share test results with the patient, but I was glad that she told me about my thyroid. The new endocrinologist did not have to prescribe any type of medication for my thyroid. I was merely instructed to get yearly checkups. So far, my thyroid is still functioning normally.

Obedience, prayer, trusting Jesus Christ and submitting to Almighty God are the keys to divine healing. The Bible says, "If you love me, you will keep my commandments" (John 14:15). God allowed me to witness and be a beneficiary of His mighty healing. First, because of obedience, God extinguished my *soul pain* to set me on a path of freedom, worship, and love for Almighty God. Second, I obeyed the instructions of God the Holy Spirit and was blessed beyond measure to see Jennifer healed to fulfill her heart's desire for marriage. Third, I was able to witness divine healing of my husband's heart. Finally, I became a first-hand witness to the miraculous healing of my thyroid. Faith allowed me to pray believing Jesus Christ would heal me and He did. What an amazing God!

These healings were accomplished by the hands of Almighty God. He will continue forever to heal His creation. God will never change. The Bible says "I the LORD do not change...." (Malachi 3:6). While the suffering body can be physically healed through medication or divine healing, Jesus Christ alone spiritually heals the suffering soul. The Bible says, "'But, I will restore you to health and heal your wounds,' declares the LORD..." (Jeremiah 30:17). There is an assurance in God's Word that healing is a result of obedience. God has shown me great and mighty things He accomplished. He is king on His throne in heaven. He is all-knowing and all-powerful. His greatness impacts my life in such wonderful ways. God blesses His obedient children, and His grace is poured out over humanity to heal the hurting soul. Practicing obedience and trusting God, results in spiritual growth that cannot be denied.

Chapter 16

Some Must Drink From the Cup

"Father, if you are willing, take this cup from me;

yet not my will, but yours be done".

(Luke 22:42)

ح‌ح‌ح‌ح‌ح‌ح‌ح

Some believers will have to drink from the cup at some point in their life. The cup is a symbol of suffering (*soul pain*). Jesus Christ had to drink from the cup of suffering. His cup of suffering was His mission on earth and can be seen in His agony in the Garden of Gethsemane, His arrest, trial, and the crucifixion. He knew the agony and humiliation He would have to endure on His way to and on the Cross. Jesus Christ knew He would suffer horrendously; therefore, Jesus prayed to His Father and asked if it was within His Father's will to remove the cup from Him, but it did not happen (Matthew 26:39). Instead, He endured the cup of suffering. The Bible says, "He himself bore our sins in his body on the tree, that we might die to sin and live to righteousness...."

(1 Peter 2:24). Not only did He drink from the cup of suffering, but His final task on earth was to die an excruciating death for the sins of humanity.

The cup of suffering may be caused by sin, loss, or other reasons. The concern is not the cause, but how believers handle the cup of suffering. The cup is not pleasant and can hold a myriad of abuses, misery, sorrow, and countless issues which bring anxiety upon the soul. Believers do not know when they will have to drink from the cup, nor do they know if it will be a long arduous experience or a short-lived occurrence. But when God's children must drink from the cup, they must look to Jesus Christ for peace in their *soul pain*. Jesus Christ's attitude while suffering displayed an absolute trust in the will of God the Father. By adopting His attitude, as revealed to believers by God the Holy Spirit, Jesus Christ provides the way to suffer without sinning. Those who suffer will not find the cup enjoyable but, gracefully, we can overcome our cup of suffering through faith in Jesus Christ. If the focus is not on Jesus Christ, the pain will continually churn in our souls. God understands the suffering of His children. He also understands that suffering can make us less self-dependent and more dependent on God for relief. Suffering exists, but there is always hope in Jesus Christ to end suffering. Through faith, Jesus Christ's suffering has brought us into a state of unity and righteousness with our all-powerful and Holy God – even in our pain.

I had to drink from the cup of suffering. God's perfect plan for my life did not include suffering, but I suffered because of sin. My cup overflowed with *soul pain*. Thankfully, *soul pain* did not define my life, nor did I live from the point of pain. The Bible says, "Many are the afflictions of the righteous, but the Lord delivers him out of them all" (Psalm 34:19). Sexual and physical abuse can be in the cup of suffering. By the world's standards, sexual and/or physical abuse victims have statistical outcomes of self-destructive behaviors, suicidal tendencies, chronic anxiety, eating disorders, sleep disorders, anger issues, bitterness, trust issues, PTSD, denial, repression, and many other long-term negative behaviors. The fact is, every sexual and/or physical abuse victim responds to abuse differently. Living life from the point of *soul pain* and not forgiving is not living the promised abundant life given by Jesus Christ. *Soul pain* is the ardent architect of invisible walls that are built around the soul causing anger and bitterness to reign behind those walls and become a way of life. Jesus Christ is the barrier against *soul pain* taking hold of the heart, mind, and soul.

Soul pain blinded me to the power of Jesus Christ for a season. Despite being blind regarding His power, I knew He shed His blood for me, and He covered my sins and immoral nature. He desires His children to have a life with Him and to have peace and harmony in their soul. In order to keep peace in my soul and a sound mind, I kept telling myself that God is my heavenly Father and Jesus Christ is my friend. Those words reassured me, and I was able to lean on Jesus Christ's strength. I did not allow myself to become mentally stagnate, live from the point of hurt, or just exist as the good things in life passed me by. The Bible says, "For my yoke is easy and my burden is light" (Matthew 11:30). There is no burden in life that is too hard for Jesus Christ to carry for me. He wanted me to have joy in being alive. The Lord delivered me from my afflictions and His grace gave me the desire to make an impact in this world and bear good fruit. My dream was to do what was right in God's eyes. As a young child, I had to make adult choices on how I was going to live my life and who I was going to live for. I chose Jesus Christ to be my refuge and my guide for relief. Jesus Christ wanted me to bring all my troubles and tribulations to Him for release, and rest for my weary soul. He allowed me to forgive myself because of the things I endured as a young child. People carry the burden of shame that can cause *soul pain*. Forgiveness sets things right in the soul. Thank the Lord, my cup of suffering did not last.

Those who suffer may feel empty inside because of *soul pain* or alienated by family members, and friends. Prayerfully, they will remember that Jesus Christ is revealed in them. The Bible says, "We always carry around in our body the death of Jesus, so that the life of Jesus may also be revealed in our body" (2 Corinthians 4:10). The disciples of Jesus Christ suffered greatly and God supplied all of their needs. Of the twelve disciples, Satan was successful with only one of the disciples, Judas Iscariot. The rest held on to Jesus knowing Him to be their savior. As our savior, Jesus Christ will supply our needs in the midst of chaos and suffering. During these times, Satan tries to rob believers of their relationship with Jesus Christ, but believers who stand on the Word of God will not be moved knowing that the cup of suffering has no permanent power.

Accepting love, counsel, and spiritual wisdom from God the Holy Spirit enabled me to realize that I was not a casualty of the war of unspeakable abuse. I am a victorious believer. Further, forgiveness allowed me to be healed to wholeness and delivered from self-destruction. The Bible says "Therefore, there is now no condemnation for those who are in Christ Jesus" (Romans 8:1). God's Word states that I should not be ashamed of my past or what others had done to me. His word consistently removes any thoughts of shame that may hang over my life and the lives of all who have suffered. The Bible says, "I sought the LORD, and he answered me; he delivered me from all my fears. Those who look to him are radiant; their faces are never covered with shame" (Psalm 34: 4-5). The Lord will carry the believer and their hurt, shame, depression, loneliness, weak faith, or whatever may be separating the believer from joy in the Lord.

When we see Jesus Christ through eyes of faith, the shame is removed and we can see our Heavenly Father. When we see Jesus Christ through eyes of faith, the brokenness is made whole and we can see heaven. Jesus Christ gives sufferers reignited hope and a relationship with Almighty God through discipleship. The Bible says, "You are the light of the world. A town built on a hill cannot be hidden" (Matthew 5:14). Believer's light for Jesus Christ can shine through suffering and suffering humbles the heart to empathize with others that suffer.

When I drank from the cup of suffering, *soul pain* became a part of my life, but God did not allow it to seize my life. I am who I am because of Jesus Christ and not because of anything I did. I am determined to use the suffering in my life to illuminate Jesus Christ in this dark world. The Bible says, "….let your light shine before others, that they may see your good deeds and glorify your Father in heaven" (Matthew 5:16). God can be glorified through every cup of suffering.

As a citizen of heaven, I am to be seasoned with grace and willing to share the truth of God's Word while doing good. Being obedient to the gospel of Jesus Christ permitted me to heal. Likewise, our loving Father will deliver His children from suffering, bondage, and depravity to become more like His Son, Jesus Christ. The cup of suffering will never deter what Almighty God has ordained the sufferer to become.

Chapter 17

A Season of Life

"and the dust returns to the ground it came from, and the spirit returns to God who gave it". (Ecclesiastes 12:7)

સ‍ેસ‍ેસ‍ેસ‍ેસ‍ેસ‍ે

God the Holy Spirit, my spiritual teacher taught me spiritual things of God. With spiritual maturity, I was able to understand that just as I was a victim of the adversary (Satan), my parents were his victims as well. Satan was the master manipulator of the abusive tactics which enslaved my parents for a long time. Satan blinded them to God's goodness and urged them towards destruction. Sadly, they were active participants of Satan's goal to destroy. They chose to live out the corruption in their hearts driven by lustful depravities, and damaged feelings and emotions. Therefore, being victims did not exempt my parents from responsibility or accountability for their actions. Forgiveness from Jesus Christ was available to them if they only asked, but the consequences were their own.

Spiritual wisdom allowed me to realize my parents were Satan's tools he wielded in a failed attempt to destroy my spiritual life. Job 1:8 says, "Then the LORD said to Satan, Have you considered my servant Job? There is no one on earth like him; he is blameless and upright, a man who fears God and shuns evil." Job was an example of spiritual strength during times of adversity. Satan's objective was to prove Job would eventually give up and abandon God. Today, Satan still seeks people for spiritual destruction because of their love for God. He delights in their heartache, *soul pain*, and sorrow. Likewise, his objective was to turn my focus away from God so that I would live through my deceitful heart's desires and focus on my heart wrenching *soul pain*. Satan wanted to keep me bound in spiritual pain and residing in spiritual bankruptcy, but he did not prevail.

To an outsider with natural eyes my family may have appeared to be a typical family. However, God saw brokenness. Though broken, my primary focus was my relationship with Jesus Christ. At the height of my *soul pain,* He transformed my heart to allow me to love my parents despite abuse. Love and forgiveness toward those that hurt me was necessary for me to be the person that God wanted me to be.

For years my mother refused to acquire the necessary skills to live independently. After years of caregiving, I could no longer provide the adequate care she needed. She required 24-hour supervised care. After researching and visiting senior care facilities, I moved my mom into a domiciliary care facility in 1986. I was comfortable with the provider and the care she received. After years in the domiciliary care facility my mother had a stroke, and the facility could no longer care for her. She was relocated to a nursing home in 2006. The nursing home was located close to my home. The owner and her daughter were very conscientious about their residents. I was satisfied with the care my mother received at the nursing home. Over the years, my mother remained physically healthy, but her sight was already damaged and she began to lose her hearing.

On a few occasions, my mother was admitted to the hospital. Hospital staff would always commend the care my mother received at the nursing home facility. They expressed that it was rare to see a long-term nursing home patient's skin in such remarkable condition. Every time my mother's condition was complimented, I would tell the owner what the hospital staff said and that I would gladly recommend their nursing home to other families.

My mother had a severe stroke in 2012, which left her unable to swallow, eat by mouth, or speak. She was tube fed thereafter. When asked a question, she responded by blinking her eyes. On Tuesday May 12, 2016, she was admitted into the hospital because of breathing problems. A CAT scan revealed she had metastatic cancer. Cancer had metastasized throughout my mother's body and I was told she would only live for a short period. Cancer was identified in her colon, liver, lungs, and lymph nodes. The oncologist wanted to perform a biopsy to determine if the colon was the primary site of the cancer, but I refused the procedure because knowing the primary site would not cure my mother's cancer and I did not want her to endure any further pain with a useless surgery. She was discharged from the hospital the same day and sent back to the nursing home. She died on May 24, 2016 at 82 years of age. My mother died as I am writing this book. I am sad about her death, but not crushed in my spirit.

Through God's grace and honoring my mother, I visited my mother both in the domiciliary care facility and nursing home to make sure she was comfortable and safe. My focus was to obey God's Word. I was told by an individual that if his parents had done to him what my parents had done to me, he would have abandoned them. The Bible says, "Honor your father and your mother, so that you may live long in the land the LORD your God is giving you" (Exodus 20:12). God's Word also says He will deal with each person according to how he/she lives and treats others. I was concerned about how God would look at me if I abandoned my mother.

Waiting at the nursing home before the funeral director picked up my mother's body, I went to her room. She looked as though she was sleeping. I thanked God for the peace He had given me at my mother's death. I was glad my mother was no longer in pain. I was blessed to have had a mother for so many years. To celebrate her life, I will purchase a biodegradable memorial tree urn to place my mother's ashes. I selected the Tulip Poplar Tree that will be planted in our back yard. This is a beautiful tree that will grow approximately 80'. As the tree grows, whenever I leave my house it reminds me of my mother. On my way home I frequently pass the nursing facility and I think about my mother. I no longer have a reason stop to talk with the staff who cared for my mother or go upstairs to visit her. I no longer sit at my mother's bedside and read scripture to her or do my schoolwork, but I yet honor her.

Everyone is created by God and should be treated with respect. People live on earth for only a short time and when the death of a loved one comes, it too can cause *soul pain.* Relatives or friends of the deceased may hurt so deeply that the death changes their lives. They cannot get back to normal patterns of living. The pain of loss can create *soul pain* deep in the crevices of the soul. It may be difficult for relatives or friends to release their loved ones and let them go. But one must remember, there is a time for everything under the sun . . . including death. It is inevitable. The Bible says, "Let not your hearts be troubled. Believe in God; believe also in me" (John 14:1). Therefore, we do not have to fear death nor be dismayed by it. Yes, the sorrow because of death can be overwhelming; however, belief in God brings peace. Praise God for the peace God gave me in my heart when my mother died. The Bible says, "Peace I leave with you; my peace I give you. I do not give to you as the world gives. Do not let your hearts be troubled and do not be afraid" (John 14:27). It was a calming peace. My mother's death was the end of a season in my life, but as one season ends, a new season begins.

The Bible says, ".... God's love has been poured into our hearts through the Holy Spirit, who has been given to us" (Romans 5:5). Everyone desires to be loved and appreciated and since believers have freely received God's love, we should freely give love to others. Simply put, God wants believers to treat people kindly. Whatever makes people suffer, be it self-inflicted, abusive relationships, illness, or anything that takes their focus from God, God the Holy Spirit can refocus sufferers toward Jesus Christ by using believers to be displays of His love and kindness. In this way, Jesus Christ can deliver sufferers from their pain to the glory of His Father.

There are seasons in which God allows things to happen in believers' lives as well. He uses those seasons to purge believers from sin, promote closeness with Him, enhance life's journey, and to learn His truths. When those seasons come, Believers must remember we have a Father who knows His children's pain and will never leave or forsake them. My season of heartache and abuse changed into a season of love and kindness. My season of caregiving ended, and a season of spiritual introspection began. My season of having a parent ended and a new season of life began.

Chapter 18

God's Transforming Love and A Transformed Life in Jesus Christ

"This is love: not that we loved God, but that he loved us and sent his Son as an atoning sacrifice for our sins". (1 John 4:10)

☙☙☙☙☙☙

God's Transforming Love

God's love was my invitation to the cherished treasure of salvation. As His love invited me to live in and for Jesus Christ, my heart was regenerated by God's marvelous power. The Bible says, "I will give them a heart to know that I am the Lord, and they shall be my people and I will be their God…." (Jeremiah 24:7). I wondered why and how God drew me to His Son, Jesus Christ as my Lord and Savior. It is a mystery I will never solve on this side of heaven. Yet, it is a mystery I delight in daily.

Since the evening I watched the movie *The Greatest Story Ever Told* as a young girl, my heart has never been the same. I was washed by the blood of Jesus Christ. My sins were forgiven, and I was not only recreated by God, but became a child of God. The Bible says, "Yet to all who did receive him, to those who believed in his name, he gave the right to become children of God" (John 1:12). That evening, as I watched the movie, my relationship with Jesus Christ was sealed. There was no doubt that Jesus Christ was my Savior and King. God's love descended upon my soul and totally changed the person that I was. The Bible says, "Therefore, if anyone is in Christ, he is a new creation; old things have passed away; behold, all things have become new" (2 Corinthians 5:17). *Soul pain* had its way with me for some time before God the Holy Spirit crept into places deep within my soul I never knew existed and I was filled with God's love despite the circumstances.

Soul pain sets sufferers up to plunge into a whirlwind of behaviors, which can result in resentment, hatred, mental confusion, heartache, and suicidal thoughts. The world offers false promises of well-being and inner peace. Sufferers may seek those false promises, but in the end, those promises are only illusions, which leave sufferers crying out "Lord help me." When I cried out, He did help me and by His strength I was able to combat evil thoughts, spiritual intimidation, temptation, cultural relativism, and enticement to destroy the deeds of the flesh caused by the effects of *soul pain*. Thank God the Lord hears and answers His children in their time of distress. The Bible says, "When the righteous cry for help, the Lord hears and delivers them out of all their troubles. The Lord is near to the brokenhearted and saves the crushed in spirit" (Psalm 34:17-18).

People of the world have more in common than what separates them. Almighty God is the God of all people. God gives comfort and loves all the people of the world, with all of our imperfections, we are covered by the perfection of His Son Jesus Christ. His grace is sufficient and equips believers to withstand their burdens. I was blessed to have Jesus Christ as my rock, my fortress, and my deliverer. The Bible says, "…My grace is sufficient for you, for my power is made perfect in weakness..." (2 Corinthians 12:9). God's transforming love is sufficient to heal lives tainted by *soul pain* and the resulting symptomatic behaviors which accompany *soul pain.*

Soul pain can attack believers' souls and minds with the purpose of turning them away from God, from living the Christian life required by God. Frankly, it can turn them into a bumbling mess; however, God's love brings good from evil and wisdom from foolishness. The Bible says, "You intended to harm me, but God intended it for good to accomplish what is now being done" (Genesis 50:20). Love made a way for all people of all nations to know Jesus Christ and that is the remedy for the troubled and lost soul. God's love is always transforming believers to live and love righteously. Do not underestimate the power of God's love.

Believers cannot humanly perceive the depths of how much God loves His children. When parents look at their newborn for the first-time, boundless emotions of love wash over them as new life is brought forth into the world. As parents, their urge to protect and provide for their newborn grows and solidifies. A new love relationship is created. Storge love develops affectionately between parent and child. This is the closest comparison to the depths of God's love for us. However, God the Father's love goes further than that. When a person surrenders his/her life to Jesus Christ, a new spiritual life is made alive and God showers His newborn with agape love. God's boundless love washes over the new believer and a new soul is brought into the kingdom of heaven. The Bible says, "So we have come to know and to believe the love that God has for us. God is love, and whoever abides in love abides in God, and God abides in him" (1 John 4:16). God's transforming love is poured into the heart of the believer until it overflows. No gender, physical appearance, nationality, or ethnicity is rejected. Discriminatory practices, coercion, unjust motives are never initiated in heaven. There is only unity in the body of Jesus Christ. Believers are blessed to be recipients of God's transforming love and to be transformed into the best Christian he/she can possibly become.

A Transformed Life in Jesus Christ

The Bible says, "If you declare with your mouth, 'Jesus is Lord,' and believe in your heart that God raised him from the dead, you will be saved" (Romans 10:9). Believers have outwardly confessed that they believe who Jesus Christ is and why He was sent to the world. Now they must, by the direction of God the Holy Spirit, apply the gospel to their lives daily and earnestly seek an indelible relationship with Jesus Christ. The believer's spiritual life begins with: 1) dying to self-will; 2) depending on Jesus Christ in every area of life; 3) obeying the teaching of God the Holy Spirit; 4) living a life of faith; and 5) discerning righteousness over sin.

There are times when *soul pain* is so unbearable and, in those times, the sufferer's faith is weakened because of sin and the weight of *soul pain*. Jesus Christ safeguards the believer from lurking evil. The Bible says, "But the Lord is faithful. He will establish you and guard you against the evil one" (2 Thessalonians 3:3). Satan fills the hearts and minds of people with lusts, lies, guilt, fear, and doubt. Instead of delighting in sinful thoughts or acting upon sinful desires, believers must come to Jesus Christ with their whole heart, bringing with them their problems, short comings, and flaws. Believers must surrender all to Him and become willing vessels who allow God the Holy Spirit to transform them. Jesus Christ is Lord and Savior, conqueror, and king. Jesus Christ must have absolute authority in the believer's life. We don't have to fear His absolute authority because Jesus Christ's yoke is filled with grace, holy power, and love. Jesus Christ delivers believers from the wrath and turmoil dwelling within the soul and replaces it with love and peace. The believer must not retaliate when someone betrays, abandons, or hurts them. The Bible says, ".....Vengeance is mine, I will repay," says the Lord" (Romans 12:19). Natural man's wicked nature seeks revenge with passion against any offense. In contrast, believers convey forgiveness to their foe instead of seeking revenge because of *soul pain.*

Jesus Christ asked His Father to gift God the Holy Spirit to His children. God the Holy Spirit transforms the believer by convicting, instructing, and guiding them into eternal truth and the righteousness of Jesus Christ. Jesus Christ has withstood the penalty of sin for the entire world; therefore, God does not want His children to suffer pain or hurt. Instead, God desires that His children live transformed lives in Jesus Christ through God the Holy Spirit. The transformed life of a believer is not without trials and tribulation, but the attitude in which those trials and tribulations are handled is witnessed by Almighty God. The Bible says, "For we are God's handiwork, created in Christ Jesus to do good works, which God prepared in advance for us to do" (Ephesians 2:10).

A transformed life in Jesus Christ will be recognized by the believer because of changes on the inside, while others will recognize changes in the believer from the outside. The transformed life in Jesus Christ changes the desires of the heart to do what is honorable, instead of ungodly acts the sufferer use to do. As effects of *soul pain* begin to diminish, the believer that yields to a transformed life in Jesus Christ starts a new way of living, a new way of thinking, and a desire to do what is right. The transformed in Jesus Christ can stand on the Word and Promises of God. The Holy Word offers transformed believers many wonderful promises that they can depend on.

Promises of God to His Children:

1. Yet to all who did receive him, to those who believed in his name, he gave the right to become children of God. John 1:12

2. For the Lord your God goes with you; he will never leave you nor forsake you. Deuteronomy 31:6; Hebrews 13:5

3. God knows the number of hairs on your head. Luke 12:7

4. The LORD hears his people when they call to him for help. He rescues them from all their troubles. Psalm 34:17

5. For I know the plans I have for you," declares the LORD, "plans to prosper you and not to harm you, plans to give you hope and a future. Jeremiah 29:11

6. God will meet all your needs according to the riches of his glory in Christ Jesus. Philippians 4:19

7. God loves you with an everlasting love. God has drawn you with unfailing kindness. Jeremiah 31

8. God works all things together for the good of those who love Him, who are called according to His purpose. Romans 8:28

9. Instead of your shame you will receive a double portion, and instead of disgrace you will rejoice in your inheritance. Isaiah 61:7

10. The LORD will fight for you; you need only to be still. Exodus 14:14

11. Call on God, and He will answer. God will be with you in times of trouble. He will deliver you and honor you. Psalm 91:15

12. Know that the LORD has set apart his faithful servants for himself. Psalm 4:3

13. I will give you a new heart and put a new spirit in you. Ezekiel 36:26

14. If God is for us, who can be against us? Romans 8:31

15. I will keep you from stumbling until you stand joyfully blameless in my presence. Jude 1:24

16. Jesus Christ promises eternal life to those that trust Him. 1 John 2:25

Promises about Jesus Christ:

17. For God so loved the world, that he gave his only Son, that whoever believes in him should not perish but have eternal life. John 3:16

18. And we have seen and testify that the Father has sent his Son to be the Savior of the world. 1 John 4:14

19. And there is salvation in no one else, for there is no other name under heaven given among men by which we must be saved. Act 4:12

20. Therefore, if anyone is in Christ, the new creation has come: The old has gone, the new is here! 2 Corinthians 5:17.

21. I will build my church, and the gates of Hades will not overcome it. Matthew 16:18

22. Jesus Christ calls us His friends. John 15:15

23. I will give you the keys of the kingdom of heaven; whatever you bind on earth will be bound in heaven, and whatever you loose on earth will be loosed in heaven. Matthew 16:19

24. If we confess our sins, He is faithful and just to forgive us our sins and to cleanse us from all unrighteousness. 1 John 1:9

Promises About God the Holy Spirit

25. Behold, I am sending forth the promise of My Father upon you, God the Holy Spirit. Luke 24:49

26. When the Helper comes, whom I will send to you from the Father, that is the Spirit of truth who proceeds from the Father, He will testify about Me. John 15:26

27. Repent, and let every one of you be baptized in the name of Jesus Christ for the remission of sins; and you shall receive the gift of God the Holy Spirit. Acts 2:38

28. When God the Holy Spirit comes, He will convict the world concerning sin, righteousness, and judgment. John 16:7-15

29. We receive the promise of the Spirit through faith. Galatians 3:14

30. You were sealed in Him with God the Holy Spirit of promise. Ephesians 1:13

Promises Directed to the Sufferer

31. Many are the afflictions of the righteous, but the Lord delivers him out of them all. Psalms 34:19

32. Blessed are the poor in spirit, for theirs is the kingdom of heaven. Matthew 5:3

33. For I consider that the sufferings of this present time are not worth comparing with the glory that is to be revealed to us. Romans 8:18

34. Blessed are those who are persecuted because of righteousness, for theirs is the kingdom of heaven. Matthew 5:10

35. Rejoice and be glad, because great is your reward in heaven. Matthew 5:12

36. Nothing will be able to separate us from the love of God in Christ Jesus our Lord. Romans 8:39

37. You have an everlasting inheritance that can never perish, spoil or fade. This inheritance is kept in heaven for you. 1 Peter 1:4

38. Seek the Kingdom of God above all else, and live righteously, and he will give you everything you need. Matthew 6:33

God's promises to His children are everlasting from generation to generation. His Words are alive, loving, and transforming. I had to rely on the promises of God to deliver me from *soul pain*. It is a blessing that *soul pain* did not destroy my relationship with God. Instead, I passionately became dependent upon and sought-after Jesus Christ for help to relieve the pain deep within the crevices of my soul. God transformed me to live a life in Jesus Christ and gave me a heart to be kind to others. The

Bible says, "And we all, with unveiled face, beholding the glory of the Lord, are being transformed into the same image from one degree of glory to another. For this comes from the Lord who is the Spirit" (2 Corinthians 3:18). A transformed life in Jesus Christ is a lifelong process, and the process is worthwhile. Those of whom God transforms are transformed undeniably. The transformed life in Jesus Christ will not think, nor will the eyes see life from a purely natural perspective ever again.

Much More To Come

As a child, spiritual brokenness and sin was all around me. My parents yielded to iniquity, but through Jesus Christ, there was hope for my situation. God spoke to me through His spirit and instructed me how I must live in this world. I was warned not to succumb to my parents' sin and that vengeance was God's alone. After all I had gone through, my *soul pain* was eliminated and the certainty of the existence of God was confirmed. Jesus Christ set me free to have peace in my soul and enjoy the world God created.

Soul pain was defeated and in my coming of age, self-centeredness and selfishness caused me to overlook the mighty hand of God for a season. The selfish part of my nature sought to go its own way. Invulnerability seeped into my heart and mind. There was no spiritual wisdom in my young adulthood. The Bible says, "Do not conform to the pattern of this world, but be transformed by the renewing of your mind…" (Romans 12:2). I was too foolish to remember that if I ignored God's Word, negative implications would take place in my life. However, Jesus Christ remained ever so close to me while I wandered as a Carnal Christian in the wilderness of the world, desiring things of the world.

As I spiritually matured, I found my way back to God with an attitude of humility, gratitude, and thankfulness. Life became sweeter than ever. The bitterness of my life has not been forgotten, but the torment and the anguish of *soul pain* has been totally removed by the mighty power of the Godhead. God gave me a living example of holiness and a precious Savior. He gave me guidance from a loving and patient comforter, God the Holy Spirit. I was released from bondage to be one with Jesus Christ and the pain I suffered does not define my life. My future looks bright.

God desires me to obey his commandments consistently. In return for obedience, He brought health and healing to my body. The Bible says, "My son, do not forget my teaching, but keep my commands in your heart, for they will prolong your life many years and bring you prosperity . . . This will bring health to your body and nourishment to your bones" (Proverbs 3:1-2, 8). As God the Holy Spirit instructed me to live a righteous life, I no longer wanted to operate outside of God's instructions. If I did, how could I expect to reap the benefits of His blessings proclaimed in the Bible.

Many things occurred in my life that I did not understand, but I had to accept what transpired. I was surprised when God chastised me in the hospital, but as a good Father, He knew I needed discipline for correction. God promised me that there is *much more to come* in my life and in the life hereafter. As my relationship with Jesus Christ grew, I realized God was in control of my life and I was not.

Part Three

Everyone Needs the

Savior - Our Lord

Jesus Christ

The Most High Dwelling Place

Above all, God wants believers to make His kingdom our dwelling place. Imagine being able to continually commune with God in loving fellowship as Adam and Eve did in the Garden of Eden. The Bible says, "Whoever dwells in the shelter of the Most High will rest in the shadow of the Almighty God" and "If you say, 'The LORD is my refuge,' and you make the Most High your dwelling, no harm will overtake you, no disaster will come near your tent" (Psalm 91:1, 9, 10). Upon welcoming believers as new children into His Kingdom, God the Holy Spirit leads, teaches, guides, and directs believers to live lives in God's will on earth, while preparing us to live glorious lives in heaven. Following His leading grants us access to dwell in His presence.

Believers make choices every day. From the time we open our eyes in the morning to start a new day, until we close our eyes at night to rest our weary bodies from the hustle and bustle of a busy day we are making decisions. In all decision making, believers must choose faith in Jesus Christ our Savior and Protector because Jesus Christ alone can make our dwelling place with His Father, Almighty God. Thinking with the mind of Jesus Christ, believers can live lives of righteousness with our family, friends, on our jobs, and in life in general. To adopt the mind of Christ, believers must intentionally grow in spiritual wisdom, which nourishes the body, and soul. Further, we must rely on the absolute truth of God's Word. When we do, the temptations of Satan will not reign in believers' lives. The Bible says, "Have I not commanded you? Be strong and courageous. Do not be afraid; do not be discouraged, for the LORD your God will be with you wherever you go" (Joshua 1:9). Instead of living a life of mistrust, worry, hurt, and insecurity, believers are assured through Jesus Christ that we have a dwelling place with Him forever.

Don't be dishearten because of internal or external suffering, God is all-sufficient, omniscient, omnipotent, and omnipresent. There is nothing too difficult for Almighty God. Meditate on the things of God day and night. Give thanks and praise Him in all circumstances. Dwell in His peace, love, forgiveness, grace, and mercy and see divine miracles appear in life.

God's people shall see all of God's promises fulfilled in due time. In God's *most high dwelling place* there is hope, love, and security. He can take all of our *soul pain,* suffering, misery and turn it into joy.

Chapter 19

Suffer God's Way

"Therefore, let those who suffer according to the

will of God commit their souls to Him in doing good,

as to a faithful Creator". (1 Peter 4:19)

ৡৡৡৡৡৡ

The Sufferer

Soul pain can have a crippling effect on sufferers. Life can become so difficult that sufferers cannot feel any delight or joy. Instead, all they feel is pain as they frequently relive incidents of *soul pain* in their minds. As a result, their lives become stagnant. Sufferers often become stuck at the point where the hurt began, and are either unable or unwilling to move on in life. They are not able to give their *soul pain* to Jesus Christ as He asks. Consequently, sufferers sometimes make *soul pain* their home and reside there. The Bible says, "For the mind that is set on the flesh is hostile to God, for it does not submit to God's law; indeed, it cannot" (Romans 8:7). Some sufferers may even feel they are alone, or in a grave situation with no means of escape. Sufferers feel the weight of the world upon their shoulders. Some conclude that desperate situations call for desperate measures. With that line of thinking, sufferers do not reason sensibly and ignore the Lord's call. But, only Jesus Christ can cure this spiritual ailment called *soul pain*.

Not thinking rationally, sufferers will often think ungodly thoughts and many times act on those thoughts to ease their pain, thereby creating damaging behaviors such as self-hatred, alcoholism, abuse of legal or use illegal drugs, sexual immorality, pornography, and other addictions in an effort to obtain healing from the haunting effects of *soul pain*. Sadly, sufferers may even contemplate suicidal thoughts in a effort to rid themselves of the incessant pain they feel. Acting on sinful thoughts, enslaves sufferers and destroys their soul. The Bible says. "The Lord—knows the thoughts of man, that they are but a breath" (Psalm 94:11). Sufferers must remember: God knows every thought they will have before it comes to mind and He is willing to be a light in those dark places.

Our thought life establishes our reality. Rehearsing negative thoughts establishes us in a dangerous reality. Out of fear, sufferers may yield to those negative thoughts, causing further pain and alienation. Not being strong in the faith, the grip of *soul pain* can cause even the righteous to become uncertain. Instead of receiving or accepting good counsel from the Word of God, believing sufferers accept contradictory counsel that does not align with God's will. Instead of relying on faith, believing sufferers rely on their emotions.

Unidentified or misinterpreted *soul pain* can be an albatross around the neck of sufferers. *Soul pain* is not always horrific, nevertheless, it can create persistent strongholds in the lives of those who suffer. *Soul pain* can drive sufferers to pursue sin to ease *soul pain.* The Bible says, "Everyone who sins breaks the law; in fact, sin is lawlessness" (1 John 3:4). *Soul pain* can be an unwelcomed agent of sin or life altering events. Regardless of the cause, sufferers' souls hurt even more when they turn from God and Satan delights to be the owner of their hurting soul.

Instead of turning from God, immense suffering should make believing sufferers come to the end of themselves, totally depending on God for relief. For that to happen, believing sufferers must adopt the proper attitude while suffering. This attitude is revealed to them by God the Holy Spirit who fully understands humanities sufferings because Jesus Christ experienced suffering while on earth. Therefore, when sufferers follow Jesus Christ's way of suffering and allow Him to be the center of their lives, they are suffering God's Way. Jesus Christ suffered physical, emotional, and spiritual trauma, but through it all He never sinned, spoke any unwholesome words, or lashed out at any of his accusers.

Transformed

Jesus Christ's suffering is the foundation of Christianity. His suffering on the cross changed the world. When God's glory comes upon our lives, we are forever changed. Suffering will always exist, but there is always hope in Jesus Christ. This hope began before the foundation of the world and will continue throughout eternity. The Bible says, "And hope does not put us to shame, because God's love has been poured into our hearts through God the Holy Spirit who has been given to us" (Romans 5:5). God wants Satan to be defeated in the lives of His children and for Jesus Christ to be their King. Therefore, God will lovingly deliver man from suffering and the depravity of bondage through faith in His Son. Jesus Christ brings the believer into a state of righteousness, and a glorious connection with an all-powerful and Holy God. Sufferers must humble themselves only to God. The Bible says, "I appeal to you, brothers, by the name of our Lord Jesus Christ, that all of you agree, and that there be no divisions among you, but that you be united in the same mind and the same judgment" (1 Corinthians 1:10). *Soul pain* separates, but Jesus Christ unites.

Be of good courage, Almighty God knows our struggles and has given us a way to deal with and eliminate *soul pain.* The solution to resolve desperate situations is Jesus Christ. He is the solution to every problem. Through Jesus Christ *soul pain* is not only alleviated, but totally eradicated by the power of God the Holy Spirit. The Bible says, "So do not fear, for I am with you; do not be dismayed, for I am your God. I will strengthen you and help you; I will uphold you with my righteous right hand" (Isaiah 41:10).

While some sufferers are drawn closer to God for divine healing, others become miserably unhappy and turn away from God. Those of us drawn to God will enjoy a life in Jesus Christ despite *soul pain* and, incredibly, develop the ability to suffer without sinning. If we do sin, we are convicted. When we are convicted of our sin, we cry out to the Lord for forgiveness and deliverance from our burdens. God the Father immediately hears and responds with forgiveness, but we must also forgive anyone who has harmed us and ask for forgiveness from anyone we have harmed. Suffering God's Way, we must walk in true repentance whereas: 1) our personal actions change; 2) our character is changed; and 3) there is a change in the way we think. To suffer God's Way, believers must focus on Almighty God in all things. Yes, we must recognize there is *soul pain* in our lives, but also know assuredly that there is a remedy. The Bible says, "Godly sorrow brings repentance that leads to salvation and leaves no regret, but worldly sorrow brings death" (2 Corinthians 7:10). For the tyranny of *soul pain* produces humility that leads to deliverance.

Further, we don't have to suffer in silence. We have an advocate who we access through prayer. We must pray to Almighty God through Jesus Christ without ceasing to release us from the authority of *soul pain*. — God's grace will comfort us in our most desperate moments. Grace from God is free and available to all at any time. With all of that said, there are two questions many of us will still ask about *soul pain*. First, "When *soul pain* is relieved, will I still experience other trials in life? The answer is "yes". Secondly, "When *soul pain* is eradicated, will I still experience temptation?" The answer is "yes." Trials, tribulations, temptations, and sin will always remain a negative force in the world until the second coming of Jesus Christ. But through Jesus Christ, when *soul pain* comes, we have the power and the strength to Suffer God's Way.

When the burden and heartache of *soul pain* has been eradicated from the deep cervices of the soul, a heavy weight is lifted from the soul, and we can acknowledge that Jesus Christ is our primary source of all that is good in our lives. The Bible teaches "Every good and perfect gift is from above, coming down from the Father of the heavenly lights . . ." (James 1:17). Believers can never reconcile ourselves to God. It is Jesus Christ who is the reconciler. Suffering can come from brokenness but Jesus Christ restores brokenness in the sufferer to wholeness. Jesus Christ is the beginning of all things and the end of all things. The transformation of the Christian sufferer will be undeniable. The Bible says about the Christian, "But you are a chosen people, a royal priesthood, a holy nation, God's special possession, that you may declare the praises of him who called you out of darkness into his wonderful light" (1 Peter 2:9).

It is instinctive to lash out at the person or persons who hurt us. Through God's grace believers can forgive and reestablish broken relationships. True forgiveness cannot be achieved by our own merit, but by the power of God the Holy Spirit through Jesus Christ. Our power of forgiveness is limited, but Jesus Christ has limitless power to heal, forgive, bring peace of mind, and calm the soul.

God is the creator of heaven, and earth and everything in it. He knows when and how believers will suffer and, through prayer, we will receive strength to bear up under the pressures of daily life. Through Him believers receive peace, wisdom, and knowledge. As recipients of the gifts of God the Holy Spirit, we gain godly wisdom, knowledge, and faith to *Suffer God's Way*. The Bible says, "And after you have suffered a little while, the God of all grace, who has called you to his eternal glory in Christ, will himself restore, confirm, strengthen, and establish you" (1 Peter 5:10). When believers *Suffer God's Way*, there is no need for us to ever be afraid, because we know we are never alone.

Chapter 20

The Distorted Reflection

"We are hard pressed on every side, but not crushed; perplexed, but not in despair; persecuted, but not abandoned; struck down, but not destroyed. We always carry around in our body the death of Jesus, so that the life of Jesus may also be revealed in our body". 2 Corinthians 4:8-10)

಄಄಄಄಄಄಄

The Sufferer

For some, looking at oneself in the mirror can cause grim *soul pain.* The heart becomes heavy-laden because of imperfect images seen through the bewildered eyes of suffering. The reflection in the mirror is distorted and void of the marvelous image God created. Because of the distorted reflection, sufferers tend to resent their appearance and their lives, which brings further sorrow to their souls. The reflected image can be so unsettling to the eye, it lures sufferers into a downward spiral of loneliness and despair. *Soul pain* can make sufferers extremely unhappy within their own bodies. Believing sufferers should not dishonor the body with fleshly desires. The Bible says, "Do you not know that your bodies are temples of the Holy Spirit, who is in you, whom you have received from God? You are not your own; you were bought at a price. Therefore, honor God with your bodies" (1 Corinthians 6:19- 20). The human body is a gift from Almighty God, but a distorted reflection can cause pain that descends deep into the crevices of their listless soul, ignoring the precious gift. Sadly, because of *soul pain*, sufferers may feel troubled when they look at their reflections—*Soul pain* this overwhelming can leave them feeling as if they can hardly breathe.

Sufferers become debilitated in their spirits. No believer wants to live in pain, guilt, or misery knowing God's soothing word is the remedy needed to heal their moaning soul. However, the truth of God's Word often becomes secondary to feelings and emotions. Likewise, utilization of the privilege of prayer becomes infinitesimal. The Bible says, "Anyone who listens to the word but does not do what it says is like someone who looks at his face in a mirror and, after looking at himself, goes away and immediately forgets what he looks like" (James 1: 23-24). Although God's Word may be read or heard, believing sufferers who go their own way, deny themselves the opportunity to be made whole and the opportunity to live the lives God created for them. They deny themselves the joy of living in Jesus Christ.

For these reasons, believing sufferers must depend on God's Word. The Bible says, "Every word of God proves true; he is a shield to those who take refuge in him" (Proverbs 30:5). Those suffering (believers and nonbelievers) experience spiritual warfare daily, but each rationalize and combat the warfare differently. Choosing the world's solution to relieve pain caused by a distorted reflection will result in yielding to the flesh and sinful desires that bring destruction to the mind, body, and soul. Acquiescing to the dictates of sin, encourages never ending *soul pain*.

The Bible says, "They are darkened in their understanding and separated from the life of God because of the ignorance that is in them due to the hardening of their hearts. Having lost all sensitivity, they have given themselves over to sensuality to indulge in every kind of impurity, and they are full of greed" (Ephesians 4:18-19). *Soul pain* hurts the sufferer, but the greatest suffering is the eternal separation from God.

Because *soul pain* can cause a distorted reflection does not justify committing evil before a Holy God. Two of Satan's most successful tactics against the believer is building spiritual strongholds in the believer's mind and creating enticing distortions for the eyes in an effort to deceive the believing sufferer. When strongholds take hold, the sufferer turns away from the truth of God and deception gains a firm footing in the mind. This will alter what is seen, and what is heard, and sufferers will not have the desire to obey a Holy God. Satan manipulates the minds of sufferers to see a false image in the mirror. The moment they accept what is felt and seen in rejection of God's truth, Satan takes control of their will and continues the illusion. The world says, "*seeing is believing*" and believing this statement will result in a false reality that rejects God's truth in order to adopt a distorted truth. The Bible says, "Before I formed you in the womb I knew you..." (Jeremiah 1:5). The Godhead is life itself. There are no falsehoods found in Him, only images of beauty.

Transformed

All believers are made in the image of God and His love is part of our spiritual DNA, which is beautifully created by Him. Contrary to the world, the Holy Scriptures teach believers that "*not seeing is believing.*" The Bible says, "For we walk by faith, not by sight" (2 Corinthians 5:7). Believers must not believe everything they see or hear. Instead, with the Helper – God the Holy Spirit — believers can choose to stand firm against Satan and the evil forces of deception in this world by putting on the full armor of God, exercising faith, and living by God's truth. The truth about our images is that God created us beautifully and there is no shame in any vessel God designs. When the mind, heart, and soul are on one accord with God's Word, the mirror reflects an image of beauty. God sees a beautiful sight when He looks at His children – ones who have been drawn by His love.

The distorted reflection can be corrected. It can become pleasing to the eye. The Bible says, ". . . you knit me together in my mother's womb" (Psalm 139:13). God's loving hands create a special thing when He knits each believer in the womb before they come into the world. As we develop our personal relation-ships with Almighty God, the distorted image can become indis-putably beautiful. The more our relationship with Him grows, the more we come to reflect Him. The sight of our own reflection in the mirror becomes good and right. Through faith, we come to realize our image is beautiful in the eyes of God. When we look into the mirror, we know we are precious in God's sight. Our images are one of a kind.

Further the physical bodies of believers are redeemed by the work of Jesus Christ on the cross. As previously stated, the distorted view of self can result in ungodly behavior and abuse. Often this behavior is abusive to the body as it is subjected to alcoholism, drug abuse, and sexual sin. By the power of God the Holy Spirit, our bodies can be renewed and transformed. With the sinful desires stripped away, our bodies have a chance to natural-ly recover. Supernaturally, the Lord Jesus Christ resurrects our broken bodies and gives us new life in Him.

Jesus Christ always gives believers the fortitude to overcome suffering in life if we seek Him. When believers suffer, we can still bring God all the glory. God may use the suffering of His children to: purify our sinful nature, discipline us for ungodly behaviors, or prompt us to release something we are holding. The mystery of why God uses suffering cannot be explained, but believers should be partakers in the lives that God has given us through Jesus Christ. Faith will allow us to see the beautiful image that shines bright in the mirror. Enjoy faith in Jesus Christ and be saturated in the presence of a Holy God. For God is love. God is good. God is righteous. The Bible says, "…weeping may stay for the night, but rejoicing comes in the morning." (Psalm 30:5). God's favor over believers lasts a lifetime and the distorted image is seen for what it is, a lie from the devil.

At the point of salvation, Christians become new creations in Jesus Christ. The distorted images in the mirror are of the old nature. Our new nature reflects new images in the mirror. The Bible says, "I eagerly expect and hope that I will in no way be ashamed, but will have sufficient courage so that now as always Christ will be exalted in my body, whether by life or by death" (Philippians 1:20). Believers are to magnify Jesus Christ within our bodies and keep our bodies holy. There is no shame in the image in the mirror. There may be imperfections seen in the mirror, but it is a privilege for Christians to honor Jesus Christ with our imperfect bodies. It is a privilege that the countenance reflected in the mirror is seen through the eyes of faith and through faith, we become wholly the Lord's. The way to keep the soul well is to commit the soul and body to God by honoring the body through righteousness. A strong soul loves the Lord and will know the truth.

Suffering may cause the believer to be on bended knee before God, but when prayers are not answered immediately, do not lose hope. The Bible says, "Wait for the LORD; be strong and take heart and wait for the LORD" (Psalm 27:14). While the believer waits on the Lord, God is already working on the believer's behalf. The hurting sufferer must listen to God's Word that tells them they are fearfully and wonderfully made. The flesh only lasts for a short time, but the spirit lasts for an eternity. God's Word is a mirror, revealing to humanity the depths of the soul man, the person they really are, and who they will become. The only solution to overcoming the distorted reflection is faith in Jesus Christ. Jesus Christ gives us confidence in and comfort with the person reflected in the mirror. When *soul pain* is eradicated, the sufferer can look into the mirror through spiritual eyes and see a beautiful reflection, a vessel fitted for the Master's use.

Chapter 21

Sin Abounds

"If anyone, then, knows the good they ought to do and

doesn't do it, it is sin for them". (James 4:17)

ৰ্জৰ্জৰ্জৰ্জৰ্জৰ্জ

The Sufferer

Sin originated in the Garden. The Bible says, "To Adam he said, Because you listened to your wife and ate fruit from the tree about which I commanded you, You must not eat from it, Cursed is the ground because of you…" (Genesis 3:17). After the fall in the Garden of Eden every descendant of Adam thereafter is guilty of sin. There are five distinct sins created by mankind: 1) the rejection of the Godhead; 2) rejection of the holy things of God; 3) rampant wickedness in the world; 4) the works of the flesh; and 5) the rise and rule of Satan in the personal lives of people. Because Adam sinned, death entered the world and Almighty God cursed the ground of the earth.

A dark heart is the legacy Adam left upon humanity. Sin, death, unrighteousness, selfishness, pride, rebellion, and hostility has come upon the souls of man. The Bible says, "for all have sinned and fall short of the glory of God" (Romans 3:23). Everyone is infected with the incurable disease of sin, but the act of sinning is a choice and the seduction of sin is rampant in the world. Since the Garden, man has fallen under the power and persuasion of sin. Sufferers must come to the realization that in this world there will always be issues that cause *soul pain*. However, in Jesus Christ, sufferers can overcome *soul pain* and have the peace of God.

The Bible says, "Your eyes are too pure to look on evil; you cannot tolerate wrongdoing…" (Habakkuk 1:13). To sin is evil and unrepented sin will shut mankind out of heaven. In the world, spiritual godliness is non-existent; therefore, the world perpetually lives in sin. Living in sin kills the human spirit, annihilates the soul and results in a lack of spiritual wisdom. Spiritual wisdom is godly wisdom that enables us to protect ourselves and our families from the outcomes of sin. Those outcomes include spiritual death making sin the only real barrier to the gift of eternal life offered by Jesus Christ, Lord and Savior.

People may know God's Word and appear religious in the sight of man, but their hearts are wicked. People who fall into this category are considered religious sinners. Jesus Christ's mission was to come to this world to display God's truth. The Bible says, "…In fact, the reason I was born and came into the world is to testify to the truth. Everyone on the side of truth listens to me." (John 18:37). People cannot find absolute truth, absolute rest, or absolute peace in their souls without fully trusting Jesus Christ. Sufferers must choose to honor and obey God more than dwell on their sinful desires. Without believing and applying God's truth, *soul pain* will ravish the core of their existence. Everyone will have to stand before Jesus Christ's final judgement. Each sufferer must decide if he or she will stand before Him as righteous or as one who missed the mark.

Soul pain creates havoc in the world, havoc in personal lives, and uses sin as a channel of destruction. Sin increases violence in the land by removing the abiding presence of God. Today, disputes are settled with hostility, guns, violence, and death. Loving parents (and parental figures) fear being arrested for correcting their children. The core family structure seems non-existent and has been completely vanquished in so many homes. The bottom line is there is death in society when wickedness becomes acceptable. The Bible says, "The Lord saw that the wickedness of man was great in the earth, and that every intention of the thoughts of his heart was only evil continually..." (Genesis 6:5). There is spiritual death when Satan's modus operandi employs lies to acquire as many souls as he can to keep mankind from being drawn to Almighty God.

Sin corrupts the soul of a man. It persuades the sufferer to submit to Satan's intentional will to control their speech, thoughts, and actions. Acting upon the demand of sin has devastating consequences. C. S. Lewis' "*Screwtape Letters*" depicts spiritual warfare and temptation by Satan and his demons on a naïve human being. A senior demon gives a junior demon, various methods to make the patient (the naïve human being) sin and eventually go to Hell. *"Your patient has become a Christian. In the meantime, we must make the best out of the situation. There is no need to despair; hundreds of these adult converts have been reclaimed after a brief sojourn in the Enemy's camp and now they are with us."* (2) The book is fictional, but the plot is an example of how eerily human beings can be manipulated in spiritual warfare by Satan and his hierarchy of demons.

The Bible says, "Jesus replied, "Very truly I tell you, everyone who sins is a slave to sin" (John 8:34). The unbeliever is a Sin Slave, a person who is the property of Satan and obeys Satan's will. The Sin Slave is under Satan's dominion and is comfortable executing *soul pain* and having sinful thoughts, sinful desires, sinful intentions, sinful habits, and sinful actions. They are workers of iniquity and devious workers of wickedness. They take delight in the pleasure of sin. They live and die in eternal damnation and death separates them from God.

They refuse to surrender to Jesus Christ as their Savior. Sin abounds in their lives. The Bible says, "All of us have become like one who is unclean, and all our righteous acts are like filthy rags; ..." (Isaiah 64:6).

Sin, rebellion, and temptation can be linked back to the Garden of Eden. Sin profits from spiritual weaknesses in humanity. The lack of trust in the Godhead puts miscreancy into action. The Bible says, "For everything in the world — the lust of the flesh, the lust of the eyes, and the pride of life — comes not from the Father but from the world" (1 John 2:16). When sin abounds in the flesh, the heart is corrupted. Lust of the flesh exhibits immoral actions: fornication, adultery, sexual perversion, incest, drinking, gluttony, drug abuse, hedonistic lifestyles, and all lusts that satisfy the flesh instead of honoring the body and a Holy God. Lust of the eyes exhibits immoral actions: consumption of pornographic material, an insatiable desire to acquire material possessions, or acquire things that don't belong to the believer. The pride of life exhibits selfish actions: exultation of self by self, arrogance, egoism, rebellion, and wanting to be served rather than becoming a servant. The pride of life is the blind desire for things of this world. All of these actions are sinful. Every kind of sin committed deserves death. Without Jesus Christ the sinner will face final judgment and punishment.

Sin is transgressions against Almighty God, unbelief in the Godhead, false teaching, and abandonment of biblical values that were once widely honored and affirmed. In the past, the earth was corrupt, and full of violence before Almighty God. Today the earth is filled with even more corruption and violence. The holy temple has become disdained instead of being honored and revered. There were church schisms in the past as well as today. Schisms can be seen in the modern Christian church because of swift changes in church doctrine such as: denying the inherent sin nature of humanity; denying God's inspiration on and His authority within Holy Scripture; denying the necessity of teaching both the Old and New Testaments in worship service; endorsing same-sex marriage and civil unions; emphasizing feminism; allowing homosexual leadership. With the abandonment of sound doctrine, some churches have become entertainment venues instead of hospitals for the soul. The Bible says, "The Spirit of the Lord is on me, because he has anointed me to proclaim good news to the poor. He has sent me to proclaim freedom for the prisoners and recovery of sight for the blind, to set the oppressed free, He has sent me to proclaim freedom for the prisoners and recovery of sight for the blind, to set the oppressed free" (Luke 4:18). Some Christians may disagree on sinful issues, but God's Word outlines what sin is and the church is where the sin sick soul can be cured.

Sin abounds in everyday life. Foul language has become an acceptable form of speech. Negative music lyrics promote gangs, guns, general violence, violence against police, and the degrading of women. The lyrics seem to justify the brutality rendering it acceptable. There is a rise in mass shootings and violence in schools. Instead of engaging in meaningful conversations, people are settling arguments with guns. There appears to be no regard for the God created human life. The Bible says, "The LORD examines the righteous, but the wicked, those who love violence, he hates with a passion" (Psalm 11:5).

Today, social media determines society's dress code, how individuals should live, and is the source of untrustworthy news. Human beings are considered things instead of the individuals God created. Authority is not respected. Young people are committing suicide because of cyberbullying and the pressures of life. People are overdosing on drugs every day. Sex and violence are glamorized in movies, on TV shows, and on the internet. Children easily obtain and are exposed to unsuitable online content at incredibly young ages. People own one or more cell phones and because of it, human interaction has changed. The desired manner of communication for young people is through text messages. Verbally talking to another person has become outdated.

The world is inundated with electronic devices and social media platforms. Because of it, there is an urgency among young people to have an instant and continuous link to each other for fear they will miss out on what's going on online or not be informed with the latest gossip of the day. Human trafficking is conducted instantly online every day. People wear very provocative outfits revealing parts of the body that should never be seen by others. The Bible says, "In like manner also, that women adorn themselves in modest apparel..." (1 Timothy 2:9). Modesty is not just clothing worn on the body, but how believers think of themselves in Jesus Christ. Christians do not need lustful attention brought to them nor should they boast about wearing name brand clothing. Almighty God and the deity of Jesus Christ are being scrubbed away from society because they are being designated as offensive. God's Holy Word is becoming identified as hate speech. Rationally thinking through issues before judgement and gathering facts has become useless in society. Emotions, feelings, hyperbolic language are what is trusted and has become the moral compass for individuals in society today. Instead of God's Word being held as the absolute truth, many are promoting their truth to power, and their reality as the sole truth in their lives. All of these faithless things are sin, sin abounds in the world, and all sin goes against a Holy God.

Soul pain can cause sufferers to live in a state of sin and in denial of their circumstances. When sufferers experience abuse, they may harm themselves, attack innocent victims, or even hurt the people they love. Because of *soul pain*, sinful acts are committed in an effort to ease the pain. The Bible says, "I do not understand what I do. For what I want to do I do not do, but what I hate I do" (Romans 7:15). Sufferers sometime say and do things that they are sorry for later. Being sorry does not excuse actions but suffering Christians must be aware that they are sinners. They must have the presence of mind that they sin every day. They must ask for forgiveness when they sin and cease to sin. When believers sin, they go against the will of God. Sin abounds in lawlessness, rebellion, and corruption of the soul. Sin abounds in humanity and forbids mankind to enter heaven. The Bible says, "Everyone who sins breaks the law; in fact, sin is lawlessness" (1 John 3:4). Praise God believers are redeemed from spiritual sin.

The Bible says, "But your iniquities have separated you from your God; your sins have hidden His face from you, so that He will not hear" (Isaiah 59:2). Before sinners give their lives to Jesus Christ and are converted, they live in darkness, are deceived by their wickedness, their hearts are wicked and deceitful, and evil is easily accepted and acted upon. The Bible says, "For you are not a God who is pleased with wickedness; with you, evil people are not welcome" (Psalm 5:4). There are many that feel they are "good people" and they are not "sinful;" therefore, they believe because they are not willfully committing sinful acts, they will enter heaven. People that think this way are fooling themselves. The Bible says, "If we claim to be without sin, we deceive ourselves and the truth is not in us" (1 John 1:8). Sin abounds in everyone's heart and God hates sin because He is holy. God's holiness, righteousness, and perfection are His being, and His Word is the absolute truth. When spiritual warfare caused by sin becomes the norm in life, it causes devastating effects on the believer and long-lasting distressing oppression upon a nation. Spiritual warfare today in the world is secularism which aims to make the things of God obsolete. To some, believing in God and the things of God are archaic and irrational.

Transformed

Sin and death entered the world through one man and tenderly, eternal life with God is granted through one man. Like *soul pain*, sin does not discriminate, no one is immune from sin, and human nature will always be sinful. Thankfully, God desires to have a relationship with sinners. He loves and blesses us despite our sinfulness because of Jesus Christ. Jesus Christ blots out the sin in the lives of believers. Only through Jesus Christ will sin be forgiven so that we can stand humbly before a righteous God. The Bible says, "He himself bore our sins in his body on the cross, so that we might die to sins and live for righteousness..." (1 Peter 2:24). "...Though your sins are like scarlet, they shall be as white as snow..." (Isaiah 1:18). The righteous blood of Jesus Christ cleanses believers from sin and appeases the wrath of God. The Bible says, "Much more then, having now been justified by His blood, we shall be saved from wrath through Him" (Romans

5:9). Only His shed blood saves us through eternity and pardons from sin.

We have all sinned and cannot stand before a Holy God. The answer is to make Jesus Christ our refuge. The Bible says, "I Trust in him at all times, O people; pour out your heart before him; God is a refuge for us" (Psalm 62:8). It is imperative to choose faith in Jesus Christ. Always walk in this life by faith because every action undertaken is seen by Almighty God. Jesus Christ lived passionately and spoke authoritatively about what was required to honor His Father and to love our neighbors. The Bible says, "…seek the Lord your God, and you will find Him if you seek Him with all your heart and with all your soul. When you are in distress, and all these things come upon you in the latter days, when you turn to the Lord your God and obey His voice; (for the Lord your God is a merciful God), He will not forsake you nor destroy you…" (Deuteronomy 4:29-31). Principalities of humanity or spiritual natures may separate sufferers from soundness of mind, good relationships, or a healthy body, but principalities cannot separate God's love from His people.

Sin that abounds in humanity causes lustful desires to rise in the soul of man. Lustful and prideful desires of the flesh can be countered by: resisting sinful indulgencies through prayer; for the lust of the eyes, guard the eyes against what is seen; and for the pride of life, change from an attitude of selfishness to an attitude of selflessness. All lust destroys the soul and should be resisted. However, resistance cannot be fulfilled by human will alone. It must be accomplished by the power of God the Holy Spirit. The Bible says, "The LORD detests all the proud of heart. Be sure of this: They will not go unpunished" (Proverbs 16:5). Pride is rebellion against a Holy God. The Bible says, "Pride goes before destruction, a haughty spirit before a fall" (Proverbs 16:18).

Some believers blame Satan for sins we commit when it is our decisions to commit the sin. There are times when God wants believers to look deeper into our lives to identify the root causes of our destructive behaviors. While investigating, believers must repent of our sins. Sadly, many of us will not acknowledge our sinfulness, depravity, faithlessness, or even our need for Jesus Christ as our Savior. God the Holy Spirit convicts the heart and produces confession. The Bible says, "If we confess our sins, he is faithful and just to forgive us our sins and to cleanse us from all unrighteousness" (1 John1:9). Believers must humbly confess our sins, depend on Jesus Christ for spiritual redemption, and depend on God the Holy Spirit to overcome the power of our sinful nature. The solution for individual and societal sin problems point to Jesus Christ. God the Holy Spirit gives the believer the ability to think with Jesus Christ to solve their problems.

Sin will always abound in this world until Jesus Christ's second coming. Suffering believers must be wise and shrewd to sin in our personal lives, sin that is in the world, and the sinful actions of others. Sin defiles human nature, it is deadly to the soul, and it corrupts the heart. Sin is sometimes the catalyst of *soul pain*, and *soul pain* has no place in the soul of man. For these reasons, humanity needs a Savior. Humanity needs Jesus Christ for our redemption and salvation. The Bible says, "But when the kindness and love of God our Savior appeared, he saved us, not because of righteous things we had done, but because of his mercy. He saved us through the washing of rebirth and renewal by the Holy Spirit, whom he poured out on us generously through Jesus Christ our Savior," (Titus 3:4-6). Jesus Christ, Lord and Savior covers our sin and sets us free. Sin that abounds in the world has no power over the believers because of the Godhead. Dependence on the promises of God, applying His Word in all areas of life, being led by God the Holy Spirit must abound in the lives of believers. The Bible says, "I consider that our present sufferings are not worth comparing with the glory that will be revealed in us" (Romans 8:18). Sin that abounds in the world has no place to thrive or survive in the hearts of believers; God's glory is revealed in our hearts.

Chapter 22

Robbery

"The thief comes only to steal and kill and destroy...".

(John 10:10)

෯෯෯෯෯෯

The Sufferer

There are societies in the world that worship false gods such as: tangible objects, mythical beings in the sky, Satan below, animals, or fictional beings created in the mind of men. None of these sources can ever spiritually connect man to Almighty God. Satan the "god of this age" is a robber. One of Satan's countless tools used to manipulate the thoughts and behavior of sufferers is robbery. Satan manipulates the truth of God's Word and his intent is to cleverly rob humanity from a precious relationship with Jesus Christ. The Bible says, "Be sober, be vigilant; because your adversary the devil walks about like a roaring lion, seeking whom he may devour" (1 Peter 5:8). Spiritual robbery encompasses many areas of the human psyche such as, youthful innocence and imagination, adolescent and teenage invincibility, and adult reasoning. All can be robbed because of *soul pain*. All can be robbed because of human weakness. When humanity is spiritually robbed, joy and peace are nowhere to be found. Robbery takes hold of the conscience, tearing families and relationships apart. Mistrust of others becomes strongholds for many. Kindness is replaced with bitterness. Cultural differences, physical appearances, and individuality that do not fit into a society's construct are frowned upon. Instead of respecting an individual's faith, religious hatred and ostracization is accepted. Biblical thinking is now seen to some as mental illness and this war on God's absolute truth robs sufferers of the desire to seek a relationship with God as well as healthy relationships with others. Doubt, loneliness, isolation, misery, and low self-esteem become "security blankets" sufferers wrap around themselves only to discover these "security blankets" inflict additional *soul pain* and despair.

Satan is spiritually felonious. He actively and diligently robs sufferers of the ability to think with reason, engage in godly decision making, comprehend the truth about the Godhead, and develop loving relationships with Almighty God. Satan robs sufferers of the joy of being alive and the delight of the gift of being a holy temple. Our bodies are not our own, but in a state of suffering, sufferers often use their bodies in many ways that are ungodly. The Bible says, "Do you not know that your bodies are temples of the Holy Spirit, who is in you, whom you have received from God? You are not your own…" (1 Corinthians 6:19). Satan is armed with an arsenal of destructive external and internal forces that continually tempt and deceive sufferers into turning away from God. Satan's continual attempts to take God's property is accomplished either by deception or by force. Deception is used as a ruse by Satan in the lives of sufferers, ensuring that sin feels gratifying when it is actually deadly. The Bible says, "For when we were in the realm of the flesh, the sinful passions aroused by the law were at work in us, so that we bore fruit for death" (Romans 7:5). This malicious ploy of Satan is executed without consent. In such situations, external forces of abuse are used through intimidation against sufferers, coaxing them to turn from God. Be clear, Satan's intent to stop humanity from seeking the truth of God's Word is premeditated and relentless. He is always ready and waiting to pounce on the weaknesses of the flesh with his lies that pervert God's truth. The robbery is complete when Satan has total control of the lives of sufferers, and they fail to seek God's help.

After the robbery, spiritual integrity rarely materializes. Instead of contemplating the gift of being temples of the Holy Spirit, sufferers have thoughts of worthlessness and feelings of not being good enough for God's love. Unconditional love from God seems to be for others. Robbed of a righteously spiritual life, it is easy for sin and lies to be accepted and, regrettably, it is difficult for sufferers to be reached with reason. The indwelling voice of God the Holy Spirit is silenced by *soul pain*: a powerful mental, physical, and emotional agent used by Satan. The Bible says, "… When he lies, he speaks his native language, for he is a liar and the father of lies" (John 8:44). The thief's (Satan) plan is for his lies to become the only truth, God's Word to become meaningless, and to destroy the whole being of sufferers.

Because of sin, Satan deceptively and successfully instigates acts of violence (in words and deeds) towards unsuspecting victims: parents, relatives, friends, or persons that have some type of influence. In such vulnerable states, sufferers may even be tricked into harming themselves. This seemingly "never-ending spiritual warfare" replaces the freedom of rejoicing in the Lord with a forlorn lingering doubt that sufferers will ever experience relief from *soul pain*. The Bible says, "But I am afraid that as the serpent deceived Eve by his cunning, your thoughts will be led astray from a sincere and pure devotion to Christ" (2 Corinthians 11:3). Further, the Bible says, ". . . Stop doubting and believe" (John 20:27). Satan always, and in all circumstances, tempts sufferers to doubt God, removing their dependance on God. This lack of dependance causes faith to diminish and be replaced by fear. Fear begins to reside as sufferers relinquish control of their lives to Satan's lies. His goal is not to merely rob sufferers of their faith in Almighty God. Ultimately, he wants sufferers to have faith in everything that dishonors God. He wants to usurp the things of God with the eventual result of God not being worshipped. Satan says of himself, "I will ascend above the tops of the clouds I will make myself like the Most High" (Isaiah 14:14). Satan wants the worship to himself.

Satan deliberately deceives humanity. He uses lies to promote what the world has to offer to supersede what God has to offer. Consequently, many find themselves trusting in what man has to say over what God says. The Bible says, "Watch out for false prophets. They come to you in sheep's clothing, but inwardly they are ferocious wolves" (Matthew 7:15). When the sufferer relys on the words of man instead of the words of God, they turn to a world of darkness and sin. Don't be like the unbeliever who enjoys sinning. The Bible says, "Do not trust in oppression, Nor vainly hope in robbery; If riches increase, Do not set your heart on them" (Psalm 62:10). Robbery is one of Satan's multitudinous schemes in his repository of weapons to deceive sufferers and encourage spiritual warfare and spiritual death. The thief's (Satan) mission is to rob sufferers of an intimate relationship with God, a healthy mind, a joyful heart, and a quiet soul by craftily seizing the possessions of God through lies, deceit, force, and mental confusion. Satan is a felonious robber, and he will always be in a relentless battle because God owns everything.

Transformed

In the face of Satan's intense desire to rob us of our walk with Almighty God, we can be transformed. If we are to experience the transforming power of God the Holy Spirit we must develop spiritual discernment. Spiritual discernment is the ability to think biblically and is a gift given to believers enabling us to see the deception of Satan from a heavenly perspective. Resisting Satan is not easily achieved without the power of God the Holy Spirit or the gift of discernment He provides. Therefore, we utilize prayer to bring Almighty God into the situation to show who He is and what He can do.

By our own strength, we cannot spiritually fight, but the battle will be won by the strength of God, our loving Father. Therefore, we must put on the whole armor of God and use each spiritual weapon in preparation for spiritual battle. The Bible says, "Put on the full armor of God, so that you can take your stand against the devil's schemes" (Ephesians 6:11). These weapons prepare us to stand against Satan's tactics and equip us with the knowledge that God provides an escape against Satan's attacks. The armor of God coupled with the power of prayer in the name of Jesus Christ combats every tactic of Satan.

God still provides for the us today and will continue to provide for us forever. While God provides, Satan simultaneously attempts to rob us of peace to bring our souls to a point of despair, but we can meet God at our point of despair. Praise God, in the court of heaven offenses committed by us in our time of suffering are forgiven because of our advocate Jesus Christ. No, Satan's crime of robbery will never be forgiven, but the power of Jesus Christ resurrects us and casts down the robber. The Bible says, "He seized the dragon, that ancient serpent, who is the devil, or Satan, and bound him for a thousand years" (Revelation 20:2). Satan has no authority over a child of God. He can only rob the soul if we allow it to happen.

Chapter 23

Is There No Relief For the Pain?

*"I have said these things to you, that in me you may have peace.
In the world you will have tribulation. But take heart; I have
overcome the world". (John 16:33)*

ॐॐॐॐॐॐॐ

The Sufferer

In the search for a means of comfort from *soul pain*, sufferers may turn to the abundant supply of counterfeit pain-relieving agents the world has to offer such as: (1) overindulgence in medication; (2) haunting behaviors; and (3) many other options to eliminate the persistent *soul pain*. These options temporarily numb *soul pain*, but do not eliminate it. Sadly, they potentially cause deeper more penetrating pain so intolerable escape by any means necessary becomes the sole intent of sufferers. Their feelings take over, logical thinking erodes, and the truth of God's Word is momentarily null and void. Counterfeit and sinful

pain-relieving agents can be found everywhere making it difficult for sufferers to press on, live by faith, or live a life according
to the will of God. The Bible says, "Who shall separate us from
the love of Christ? Shall tribulation, or distress, or persecution,
or famine, or nakedness, or danger, or sword?" (Romans 8:35).
Even in a state of confusion, God still loves sufferers.

Sufferers may become very discouraged with their state of
being because they are emotionally encased in pain. *Soul pain*
builds invisible walls within the soul as a fortress to avoid any
further pain. Those walls do not allow love to come in or out, and
the fear of pain remains in complete control. The promised abundant life is not realized. The incentive to live the promised abundant life is placed in an immobile fruitless position within inac-
cessible hearts. Sufferers become obsessed with ridding the *soul
pain* from their lives, while becoming addicted to the counterfeit
pain-relieving agents. Unknowingly sufferers become gardeners.
They water, fertilize, mulch, and prune their *soul pain* to help it
grow. When a stronghold materializes but is not spiritually addressed, the effects of *soul pain* never leave. Many times, under
the pressure of spiritual warfare, sufferers cannot search outside
of their own circumstances to seek the truth of God. The expres-
sion, "you can't see the forest for the trees" means not being able
to see the broader picture in a situation or see the destruction
that *soul pain* brings. In this state, sadly, some sufferers may not
even be aware of their *soul pain* related suffering. They do not
understand why they have seemingly lost proper judgment leaving them stripped of their dignity – humiliated, embarrassed, and
devastated. From this lowly position, they wonder why life is so
difficult. This is a trap of Satan placed in the mind by *soul pain*.

Soul pain does not choose a certain time or group of individuals to attack. Job, a prosperous and faithful man, lost everything.

He lost his wife, children, servants, good health, and possessions. He became terribly ill with sores all over his body. The Bible says, "So Satan went out from the presence of the LORD and afflicted Job with painful sores from the soles of his feet to the crown of his head" (Job 2:7). He went from living a life of faith as a respected member of his community to living a life in a garbage dump. His friends told him his tragedy was because of some sin he committed. They did not know or understand the plans God had for Job. Through all of Job's heartache, he did not blame God for his misfortune. The Bible says, "In all this, Job did not sin by charging God with wrongdoing" (Job 1:22). Instead, Job waited on God to send salvation. People say, "Let go and let God." It is such a simplistic statement to resolve life's problems, but *soul pain* cannot be simplistically cast away. When sufferers are at their breaking point in life, like Job, they must seek the salvation of the Lord. Many can relate to suffering, but Job demonstrated that though suffering may seem never ending and relief seems hard to find there is plenty of Godly wisdom to be gained through pain.

Transformed

Believers know that Almighty God is a God who sees, hears, and answers His children. As a loving Father, He answers His children in our times of distress. The Bible says, "Cast your cares on the LORD and he will sustain you; he will never let the righteous be shaken" (Psalm 55:22). God's truth and love is always available, even when the power of *soul pain* seems overwhelming. Job is an excellent example of this. Even in pain, Job was faithful. God blessed him for his faithfulness. God blessed Him with a new family and more possessions than he previously had. The Bible says, "He (God) will wipe every tear from their eyes . . ." (Revelations 21:4). Jesus Christ will solve all of our problems if we trust Him. God's plan for the lives of believers may not feel good, but God is Jehovah, He is Mighty God and He wants the best for His children. The Bible says, "You number my wanderings; Put my tears into Your bottle; Are they not in Your book?" (Psalm 56:8). As long as we live in this fallen world, there will be suffering because of sin; however, the promise of what is to come in eternity will one day be revealed to all believers and *soul pain* will be but a faint memory. "My flesh and my heart may fail, but God is the strength of my heart and my portion forever" (Psalm 73:26).

Through prayer God hears our cries. Through love He answers. His loving power is intertwined in the life of His children. God never leaves us, and Jesus Christ gives us the precise pain relief we need – internal peace. In pain, believers can find hope in God's love, hope in the advocate (Jesus Christ), and hope in the helper and teacher (God the Holy Spirit). Hope is manifested in the hearts, minds, and souls of believers. The Bible says, "It was good for me to be afflicted so that I might learn your decrees" (Psalm 119:71). Even in pain, life is full of teaching moments. In times of *soul pain*, we are taught the things of God by God the Holy Spirit and feel closest to our mediator, Jesus Christ, in our affliction. We are reminded that our lifelong friend is familiar with our darkest valley. Knowing He is in fellowship with our suffering draws us nearer to our God. The Bible says, "give thanks in all circumstances; for this is God's will for you in Christ Jesus" (1 Thessalonians 5:18). God can use heartache and sorrow for good in the lives of believers. For His glory believers' greatest hurts can be our greatest testimony if we allow Jesus Christ to step in and take our pain.

Chapter 24

Separation and Brokenness

"The LORD is close to the brokenhearted and saves those who are crushed in spirit". (Psalm 34:18)

ॐ ॐ ॐ ॐ ॐ ॐ ॐ

The Sufferer

Adam's sin is endemic to the human race condemning man forever. Consequently, humanity is spiritually separated from God at birth. Sin separates humans from God, while brokenness brings shame and isolation. Separation and brokenness are universal. Like *soul pain* they do not discriminate based on race, age, gender, religion, ethnicity, or status in life. The Bible says "...There is no one righteous, not even one" (Romans 3:10). This scripture indicates that all mankind is under the guilt of sin. All mankind is separated from God and broken before Him. Those who are broken in spirit often feel discarded, as if they are useless or can be thrown away. Their *soul pain* equates to more than broken souls, but broken minds and broken emotions as well.

Though brokenness can be the result of negative stimuli such as wrong lifestyle choices, arrogance/pride and rebellion, brokenness can also have a powerful outcome. It is in our brokenness that the choice is made to either: 1) live for God and be led by God the Holy Spirit; or 2) live to satisfy the corrupt sinful desires of the flesh and experience eternal separation. God gave humanity the tremendous gift of autonomy — the choice is theirs to make.

Separation from God and belief in ungodly worldliness/wickedness can lead to brokenness and a life that is self-destructive. Separation ushers in isolation, spiritual warfare, depression, despair, deception, selfishness, bitterness, and unending *soul pain*. The Bible says, "We all, like sheep, have gone astray, each of us has turned to our own way. . ." (Isaiah 53:6). Sinful nature and willfully sinning separates humanity from God. Sadly, when *soul pain* strikes, sufferers who go their own way find pleasure in sin. The Bible says, "A man who isolates himself seeks his own desire; He rages against all wise judgment" (Proverbs 18:1). The rebellious sinner deserves sorrow, separation, sadness, and heartache. The choice to sin keeps sufferers separated from God. The Bible says, "If you do what is right, will you not be accepted? But if you do not do what is right, sin is crouching at your door; it desires to have you, but you must rule over it" (Genesis 4:7).

The brokenness that began in the Garden of Eden was not God's plan. Remember mankind is autonomous. Adam's choices began the first broken relationship with God and brokenness has spiraled out of control ever since. *Soul pain* is brokenness in the soul of man, but there is a remedy: Jesus Christ. Jesus Christ is eternally connected with His Father. However, on the cross, Jesus Christ took on the sins of the entire world. As previously stated, sin separates humanity from Almighty God. For the first time Jesus Christ felt separation from His Heavenly Father as God Almighty's face was hidden/withdrawn from Him. It is presumed Jesus Christ felt a great sense of separation, brokenness, and silence from heaven when He was nailed on the cross. The Bible says, "...Jesus cried out in a loud voice, "Eli, Eli, lema sabachthani?" (which means "My God, my God, why have you forsaken me?" (Matthew 27:46). While on the cross, Jesus Christ's humanity was fatherless for six hours. Neither His earthly father nor His Heavenly Father were present when His humanity experienced incredible *soul pain*. What horrendous *soul pain* He went through? Jesus Christ suffered physical, mental, and emotional *soul pain* to mollify the wrath of His Father for the world's sake. Jesus Christ chose to experience *soul pain* because of love. Love for me, love for you, and love for the world. Jesus Christ made the ultimate sacrifice. The Bible says, "And being found in appearance as a man, he humbled himself by becoming obedient to death — even death on a cross!" (Philippians 2:8). His disconnection with His Father in heaven for the first time was impassioned. On the cross, Jesus Christ reached the pinnacle of brokenness and separation to fulfill His mission of taking on sin for the world. Only Jesus Christ could sacrifice His life for mankind to obtain eternal redemption and salvation. His sacrifice was mournful, but it was necessary. When Jesus Christ became the world's "sin bearer," God the Father had to turn away from His cherished Son.

Like Jesus Christ when sufferers feel separated from God it only intensifies their brokenness. Without accepting the finished work of Jesus Christ on the cross, sufferers can be sucked into a hopeless spiritual pit designed to enslave them to known and unknown wickedness in the heart. The Bible says, "The heart is deceitful above all things, and desperately wicked. . ." (Jeremiah 17:9). Brokenness because of *soul pain* can make sufferers so demoralized, that they are blinded to the light of Jesus Christ and they only see darkness.

Before choosing eternal separation and well-deserved punishment for sin, suffers must ask themselves if they truly understand the ramifications of a life without Jesus Christ? Will this begin a life of wallowing in *soul pain*? Will self-pity be their moniker? Will sin rule in all aspects of their lives? The sufferer must ask themselves these questions. Separation from God is a nightmare that never ends. Separation from God is guaranteed if sufferers refuse to develop relationships with Jesus Christ.

An Old Testament prophet said about God's people, "But your iniquities have made a separation between you and your God, and your sins have hidden his face from you. . ." (Isaiah 59:2). The prophet so poignantly spoke about our Heavenly Father as perfect, holy, righteous, and pure. No sin can be before Him. No matter the individual, everyone is spiritually dead and spiritually broken until their second birth. The Bible says, "Jesus replied, ". . . Very truly I tell you, no one can see the kingdom of God unless they are born again" (John 3:3).

Brokenness manifests itself in many forms. Being broken-hearted comes from emotional pain, or *soul pain,* that originates from Satan's assaults. Brokenness is a spiritual state of being. If allowed, brokenness created by *soul pain* can become a permanent reality. Lot and his wife were commanded by the angels of God not to look back at the destruction of Sodom and Gomorrah. Lot's wife was curious about the condition of her land and her people. She disobeyed God's command and looked back causing her death. Her death is an example of going back or desiring the former life and returning to sin. The Bible says, "But Lot's wife looked back, and she became a pillar of salt" (Genesis 19:26). Sin will always cause brokenness and sin always separates mankind from Almighty God.

There are times, Satan is blamed for *soul pain* and brokenness. However, it may be something sufferers are causing themselves. Sufferers may mask their pain and function normally in the world and among family and friends, but their souls experience something different. In contrast, sufferers may also exhibit unacceptable behaviors because of their negative experiences with *soul pain*. Sufferers demonstrating negative behaviors are branded with some type of false label (promiscuous, drug addict, lost cause), hindering them from living a life of freedom. It may also be God allowing *soul pain* to bring about changes or stop progression down a doomed path. In either sense, God wants sufferers to turn to Him for all things. It is God's omniscience that knows when chastising is beneficial and how to make it work for their good.

Brokenness because of *soul pain* can strain relationships and cause needless suffering. When problems come, a broken spirit can cause adults to act out just as children do. In these times, the sufferer may withdraw from family and friends, or display other negative behaviors. As a result, the list of labels grows longer: loser, weakling, confused, mental, weirdo, problem child. These and many other offensive labels are often placed on sufferers because they are misunderstood. These labels are NOT who sufferers are, but symptoms of what they do to ease their pain. Those who display symptoms of a broken spirit need a Savior who can give them a new identity. The Bible says, "He will wipe away every tear from their eyes…" (Revelations 21:4). The sufferer has the right to loudly and boldly cry out to Almighty God to plead for relief because of separation and brokenness.

Transformed

Only God can draw man to repentance to end separation from Him. The Bible says, "…Repent and be baptized, every one of you, in the name of Jesus Christ for the forgiveness of your sins. And you will receive the gift of God the Holy Spirit" (Acts 2:38). Repentance is mandated by Almighty God and is twofold. (1) God's conviction: God allows sin to be revealed to the soul of man; and (2) a repentant act by man asking for forgiveness of their sin. It is a provision as well as a decision. The gift of repentance from God is for man to turn away from their depravity and choose what is right and holy. Pain in the soul can be reduced or eliminated if we make the right choice, in Jesus Christ.

Those who believe in the Savior, will no longer be separated or be in spiritual darkness. They will forever be connected to the Father for eternity. Nothing can separate believers from God's love. The Bible says, "For I am sure that neither death nor life, nor angels nor rulers, nor things present nor things to come, nor powers, nor height nor depth, nor anything else in all creation, will be able to separate us from the love of God in Christ Jesus our Lord" (Romans 8:38-39). Life can be full of problems, or life can be full of peace and joy. The latter is through gifts given by Jesus Christ.

Through God the Holy Spirit, the believer can escape the broken soul and corrupt ways of the world to be brought into union with Jesus Christ. Sin no longer has dominion over us. Through Jesus Christ, there is no condemnation of past trials and tribulation or sins committed by or committed against believers. The Bible says, "Therefore if any man be in Christ, he is a new creature: old things are passed away; behold, all things are become new (2 Corinthians 5:17). For these reasons, we can live in spiritual peace, love, and joy. As believers and members of God's family, we are loved, cared for, cherished, never separated, and a treasured possession no matter our former state of brokenness.

My divine unity with Jesus Christ is profound. I will never be separated from Almighty God. This knowledge and time have healed my brokenness. I did not become a victim of brokenness or remain separated from Almighty God because of my past circumstances. I am a survivor of *soul pain* and my faith in Jesus Christ unites me with Almighty God. My spirit has been resurrected from the deadness associated with being separated from God. The life of separation ended when Jesus Christ came into my life. God's divine providence in my life overruled all the evil intentions Satan desired for me. God blessed me tremendously even in the times when I didn't deserve His blessing or when I did not follow the teachings of Jesus Christ. God will always know my brokenness, weaknesses, and failures, but He forgave and continually forgives me. Because He forgives me, I want my thoughts, what I say, and do in my life to shine as a beacon for Jesus Christ' sake.

God the Holy Spirit is a valuable gift given to me from Almighty God for my faith in His Son, Jesus Christ. He was sent to me because of love. Love enabled me to move past my *soul pain*, to love myself, and love others. Even through abuse, I was compelled by God the Holy Spirit to treat my parents with respect. I had to seek His guidance through my *soul pain*. I chose not to rebel or hate. Instead, I chose to love and be obedient to my parents so that *soul pain* would not have power over me. God the Holy Spirit sensitized me to please God in my young life. His powerful presence convicted me to know that my life was not my own. No, I did not make godly choices in all things, but I did make the godly choice to accept Jesus Christ as my savior and accept his gift of salvation from sin.

God's healing grace allows us, while broken, to encourage and uplift others out of the depths of *soul pain*. The most effective weapon against brokenness and *soul pain* is surrendering our lives to Jesus Christ. Don't look back as Lot's wife did. Don't dwell on past hurts or desires. Focus on Jesus Christ and hold on to what He will bring to the lives of believers. Applying the powerful Word of God to our lives produces spiritual wisdom. The Bible says, "For though we walk in the flesh, we are not waging war according to the flesh. For the weapons of our warfare are not of the flesh but have divine power to destroy strongholds. We destroy arguments and every lofty opinion raised against the knowledge of God and take every thought captive to obey Christ" (2 Corinthians 10:3-5). Growing in spiritual knowledge given by God the Holy Spirit invigorates the soul and does not crush the spirit. Adam's sin creates spiritual death to the human spirit and separates humanity from God. The applied blood of Jesus Christ resurrects the human spirit and rejoins it to Almighty God. The broken heart and the broken soul are mended together to a place of well-being. God's love mends our brokenness and makes us whole. From that moment every problem believers encounter has a solution, and the solution is God Almighty's precious Son, Jesus Christ.

Chapter 25

God the Holy Spirit - Power to Live By

"But the fruit of the Spirit is love, joy, peace, patience, kindness, goodness, faithfulness, gentleness, self-control. Against such things there is no law". (Galatians 5:22-23)

❧ ❧ ❧ ❧ ❧ ❧

The Sufferer

No one is exempt from *soul pain*. Even believers saved from the penalty of sin, may encounter something that causes them to suffer. Suffering believers may know God's Word, but because of *soul pain*, not have the will to apply it in their daily lives. Occasionally, suffering believers become too weak in their faith to follow instructions from God the Holy Spirit. When in this condition, they miss the spiritual power God the Holy Spirit brings. Hardships will occur in the lives of believers, but having the inability to act or outright refusing to act in accordance with the guidance of God the Holy Spirt will cause believers to stumble or fall away from their faith. The Bible says, "It would have been better for them not to have known the way of righteousness, than to have known it and then to turn their backs on the sacred command that was passed on to them" (2 Peter 2:21).

What would cause a believer to refuse God the Holy Spirit? For some, the world's lies are more inviting than the truth of God's Word. In those cases, God's Word almost seems useless in the struggle against *soul pain*. Without spiritual guidance, *soul pain* can cause believing sufferers to be conflicted in what they believe, yielding easily to the desires of the flesh instead of yielding to the grace of God. The Bible says, "Therefore do not let sin reign in your mortal body so that you obey its evil desires" (Romans 6:12). Believers are dead to sin, but they cannot stop the lure of sin to commit sinful acts. Only submitting to God the Holy Spirit can do that. Without submission there is only abdication. Believers who abdicate their power of righteousness and settle for doing what is against the will of God become encumbered by regret and sadness.

Humanity is in such a depraved state because of the sin nature. What is seen, heard, opined, or believed about societal norms, the world, people, or self can be far removed from God's ordained truth. The Bible says, "For my thoughts are not your thoughts, neither are your ways my ways, declares the LORD" (Isaiah 55:8). Some traditions and practices passed down in families, and churches are unbiblical. They are just mere traditions which, unfortunately, have nothing to do with God. Many claim to be devoted to the Lord "outwardly," but "inwardly" have corrupt hearts. There are preachers who add to their own words to alter the Word of God. The Bible says, "Thus you nullify the Word of God by your tradition that you have handed down. And you do many things like that" (Mark 7:13). Traditions can make

God's Word meaningless, increasing false philosophies and validating an "individual's reality as truth." People today say "my truth" or "truth to power" when explaining their life experiences or opinions as if it's THE truth. As a result, the rest of us must remember every person has their own journey or their own reality in life. Dismally, relativism has become an accepted standard because the premise of this theory indicates that truth is what an individual or culture believes. All of these theories are illusions of truth and are highly regarded in today's culture. These truths are held up as moral standards but are NOT truth. God's Word is the only absolute truth. With so much confusion, suffering believers can be caught up in a web of ambiguity. They have no power to do what's right or think what is right without the power of God the Holy Spirit.

Transformed

When believers accept Jesus Christ into our lives, we are immediately indwelt by the gift of God the Holy Spirit, the spiritual power of God. This power opens hearts and minds to the truth of God and the righteousness of Jesus Christ. Along with Jesus Christ, God the Holy Spirit is another precious gift anyone can receive. God the Holy Spirit provides us with spiritual power to act and react to this dark world respectfully and to the glory of Jesus Christ. When we submit to God the Holy Spirit, He humbles us to the point that we understand our need for Jesus Christ. It becomes clear that without Him we can do nothing to please God Almighty. The Bible says, "I am the vine; you are the branches. If you remain in me and I in you, you will bear much fruit; apart from me you can do nothing" (John15:5). Thankfully, God the Holy Spirit gives believers spiritual power to resist sinful thinking, ungodly speaking, sinful behavior, and rebellious lifestyles. It is obvious that human nature is corrupt, but God the Holy Spirit gives us the power not to capitulate to lust and rebellion – the corruption raging in the world.

A heightened sensitivity to sinfulness occurs as the hearts of believers are transformed. Our spirits are troubled when witnessing ungodly activities or hearing ungodliness. This is the on-going work of God the Holy Spirit crushing the lust of the flesh, the lust of the eye, and defeating the pride of life within us. Working in conjunction with God's Word and God's grace, God the Holy Spirit empowers us to defeat *soul pain* in its many forms. God's Word tells us who we are. God's grace frees us from the reign of sin and brokenness. God the Holy Spirit ignites our conscience to His Word and makes us receptive to His grace. He encourages believers to abandon wicked things and seek heavenly things. This constant work of convicting, teaching, and equipping transforms us into the likeness of Jesus Christ. God the Holy Spirit is the divine connection to Almighty God and He gives believers the power to walk by faith. The Bible says, "Therefore we do not lose heart. Though outwardly we are wasting away, yet inwardly we are being renewed day by day" (2 Corinthians 4:16).

God the Holy Spirit works in and through believers to achieve God's will. As He works, God the Holy Spirit gently and gradually removes the sting of *soul pain* until it no longer exists. God the Holy Spirit dwells within believers to prepare us for our eternal resting place with Almighty God. The Bible says, "And, behold, I send the promise of my Father upon you. . ." (Luke 24:49). As God breathed life into man at creation, Jesus Christ sends God the Holy Spirit unto those He has redeemed. Therefore, we seek Almighty God through God the Holy Spirit who dwells within all believers. The Bible says, "And if the Spirit of him who raised Jesus from the dead is living in you, he who raised Christ from the dead will also give life to your mortal bodies because of his Spirit who lives in you" (Romans 8:11).

God the Holy Spirit's loving power seeps deep into the crevices of the soul to give peace to the brokenhearted. His loving power silences the chaotic mind with a quiet calming voice instructing whoever will listen in the ways of the Lord. Through Him the believer realizes that God loves them and wants to make them whole thereby rending *soul pain* powerless.

The Bible says, "And so we know and rely on the love God has for us. God is love. Whoever lives in love lives in God, and God in them" (1 John 4:16). The Bible tells the believer that God the Holy Spirit is, Himself, a divine person. He is a being with a mind, emotions, and a will. God the Holy Spirit was part of creation, "…and the Spirit of God was hovering over the waters" (Genesis 1:2). He reveals the true wisdom of God, "these are the things God has revealed to us by his Spirit" (1 Corinthians 2:10a). He knows the deep things of God, "…searches all things, even the deep things of God" (1 Corinthians 2:10b). He has a mind, "And he who searches our hearts knows the mind of the Spirit because the Spirit intercedes for God's people in accordance with the will of God" (Romans 8:27). He teaches things that Jesus Christ spoke, "But the Advocate, the Holy Spirit, whom the Father will send in my name, will teach you all things and will remind you of everything I have said to you" (John 14:26). He intercedes for believers, "…but the Spirit himself intercedes for us through wordless groans" (Romans 8:26). He leads the children of God, "For those who are led by the Spirit of God are the children of God" (Romans 8:14). His being has emotions, "And do not grieve God the Holy Spirit of God, with whom you were sealed for the day of redemption" (Ephesians 4:30). His being has a will, "…the work of one and the same

Spirit, he distributes them (gifts) to each one, just as he deter-mines" (1 Corinthians 12:11). He dwells in the intangible heart of the believer, "Do you not know that your bodies are temples of the Holy Spirit, who is in you, whom you have received from God? You are not your own" (1 Corinthians 6:19).

Delightfully, believers receive power when God the Holy Spirit comes upon us. We are changed internally, and the power is projected outwardly honoring Almighty God. Believers are spiritual babes when we receive God the Holy Spirit, but by His power, we grow into spiritual maturity. The Bible says, "But you will receive power when the Holy Spirit has come upon you, and you will be my witnesses..." (Act 1:8). Believers have the spiritual power to: (1) face and stand up to their enemies without shame; (2) stand boldly on the Word of God; (3) profess that Je-sus Christ is their Lord and King; (4) have a renewed mind, heart, and soul; (5) be wise enough to resist Satan's assaults and temp-tations; and (6) to spiritually discern the manipulation of Satan.

Soul pain has a mighty imposing opponent, the Godhead. The Bible says, "For our struggle is not against flesh and blood, but against the rulers, against the authorities, against the powers of this dark world and against the spiritual forces of evil in the heavenly realms" (Ephesians 6:12). The fight for the soul is a spiritual manifestation, in the heavenly kingdom. The height of spiritual warfare is fought by the Godhead and is always won by His magnificent power. God the Holy Spirit will always give believers the power to withstand what is ungodly. God the Holy Spirit gives believers extraordinary spiritual power to enjoy and live abundant lives, love being Christians, love others, and to grow in spiritual wisdom.

Chapter 26

Spiritual Peace

"Now may the Lord of peace himself give you peace at all times in every way. The Lord be with you all". (2 Thessalonians 3:16)

ॐॐॐॐॐॐॐ

The Sufferer

Without direction from God the Holy Spirt, sufferers may have difficult times dealing with and responding to *soul pain*. Their minds and emotions often give way to worry, anger, bitterness, spiritual blindness, and depression. These emotions can elicit misery and heighten desires to be immersed in ungodliness. Misery induced *soul pain* drives sufferers to seek peace – spiritual peace which often seems beyond their reach. As they look around, the absence of true peace can leave them feeling hopeless and drive them to act impulsively with self-destructive behaviors. In extreme cases, to end their misery, sufferers may even contemplate suicide as the most logical solution to their despair. The Bible says, "Anxiety weighs down the heart…" (Proverbs 12:25).

Despair resulting from a lack of peace can be directly correlated to disobedience and the inability to correctly respond to *soul pain*. Additionally, despair is the result of responding to the lies of the world instead of the truth of God. The Bible says, "There is no peace," says the LORD, "for the wicked" (Isaiah 48:22). Are sufferers wicked? *Soul pain* can cause sufferers to respond to the rage within their troubled spirit with sin. The only answer to that rage is God Almighty. Therefore, sufferers must intentionally pray constantly about everything. The Bible says, "pray without ceasing" (1 Thessalonians 5:17). When sufferers think God does not answer their prayers, He is giving an answer. He is saying, "wait on the Lord." The time has not yet come for the prayer to be answered.

The world has numerous suggestions for superficial inner peace. The world's flawed methods include techniques such as: just be happy; enjoy music; play with your pet; do deep breathing/relaxation exercises; love self; set objectives for yourself; don't worry about things you cannot control; or say how you feel. These worldly processes are self-taught and not God centered. Worldly advice and worldly instruction on peace will never last.

God knows exactly what sufferers endure – in the past, present, and future. The consequences of *soul pain* causing disruption within the soul results in no peace, which has many representations. These representations can appear as: 1) anger at God because of the trials and tribulation He has allowed in the sufferer's life; 2) feelings of frustration, depression, or hopelessness with no way to rectify problems; 3) the manifestation of an abundance of self-destructive behaviors; 4) self-condemnation; 5) habitual lying to God, self, and others; 6) self-hatred; 7) despair because of the sufferer's spiritual state; and 8) unholy doubts (doubt that God hears the sufferer's cries for mercy, doubt that the agony in the soul is spiritual, doubt that God knows they exist, or doubt that God loves them). All of these representations are killers of inner peace.

Transformed

In all situations, we must thank God for everything He has done and will do for us – even in chaotic or painful matters. Our gratitude stems from the extraordinary spiritual strength we obtain from God the Holy Spirit. This strength allows believers to have peace in our souls in all matters. Our unbreakable union with God through our faith in Jesus Christ creates an unfailing inner peace. Faith and prayer not only maintain our connection to God the Father, but they also forge a path to the gift of secure peace only accessed through faith in the Lord Jesus Christ. Our faith is rewarded with true spiritual peace. Jesus Christ offers inner peace and He gives it abundantly. Living a life of righteousness affords us divine peace. Let's consider what the Bible says about peace:

1. The LORD gives strength to his people; the LORD blesses his people with peace. (Psalms 29:11).

2. Turn from evil and do good; seek peace and pursue it. (Psalms 34:14).

3. Now may the God of hope fill you with all joy and peace in believing, that you may abound in hope by the power of the Holy Spirit (Romans 15:13).

4. If it is possible, as far as it depends on you, live at peace with everyone (Romans 12:18).

5. Blessed are the peacemakers, for they will be called children of God (Matthew 5:9).

6. Let the peace of Christ rule in your hearts, since as members of one body you were called to peace. And be thankful (Colossians 3:15).

7. Make every effort to live in peace with everyone and to be holy; without holiness no one will see the Lord (Hebrews 12:14).

8. Peacemakers who sow in peace reap a harvest of righteousness (James 3:18).

Without spiritual wisdom, an issue or situation can frighten us into acting out of character. However, allowing God the Holy Spirit to control the mind and soul gives lasting inner peace as believers learn to give their problems and pain to Jesus Christ. It may be hard to do but, the Lord knows how to deal with it better than the believer possibly can. Inner peace that comes from the Godhead is comforting, quieting, and hopeful. The Bible says, "The LORD lift up His countenance upon you, And give you peace" (Numbers 6:26).

The peace that the Lord gave me changed my attitude. When I was at one of my lowest points in life, I cried out to Jesus Christ, He gave me spiritual peace and my life was changed because of it. I realized God heard my prayers. It was good to know that a loving God keeps His promises. The Bible says, "Jesus Christ is the same yesterday, today and forever" (Hebrews 13:8). Jesus Christ never changes, and He offers peace to all who are willing to receive it. It is God's peace for the soul we must seek. Embracing inner peace as the world suggests is futile and short-lived leaving the soul unfulfilled. Only Jesus Christ can deliver what the aching soul needs – divine peace.

Chapter 27

A Transformed Heart

"Keep your heart with all diligence, For out of it spring

the issues of life." (Proverbs 4:23)

ৡৡৡৡৡৡ

The Sufferer

In many cases of lingering *soul pain*, abusive family members, acquaintances, or strangers have caused suffering beyond comprehension. Sufferers are left with feelings of guilt, shame, and hatred. Hatred is a feeling that goes against God's will and makes life awkward as feeling hatred make the disbursement of love and forgiveness more and more difficult. How can sufferers love anyone, especially the wicked or loveless person/people who hurt them? To do so, goes against all human senses and the basic instinct of self-preservation. Abused hearts are not open to give love, receive love, or be kind but, due to lingering *soul pain*, remains constantly pulled as if in a tug of war between righteousness and sinfulness.

While experiencing abuse, sufferers are sometimes treated as if they allowed their abusers to continually abuse them or allowed their abusers to remain in their lives. Sufferers often feel judged. These feelings are particularly strong when others see them as complicit in their own suffering. "Why didn't you leave? Why didn't you stop them or report them?" These questions suggest that somehow the sufferer is as guilty as the abuser. The stress of this judgment, *soul pain,* and life's ordeals can break hearts driving sufferers to make wrong choices in their lives, turning the lives of sufferers upside down with worry and fear that their lives will never change.

The act of abuse in any form comes from the condition of the heart. The Bible says, "But what comes out of the mouth proceeds from the heart, and this defiles a person. For out of the heart come evil thoughts. . ." (Matthew 15:18-19). Because of *soul pain*, sufferers may think evil thoughts and do wicked things they regret. Further, because of abuse, sufferers may see themselves as irredeemable having weakened faith, or no faith at all. Accordantly, sufferers find themselves in an endless cycle of spiritual pain (It is claimed that the thing sufferers have been victimized of in their young life, will become a stronghold in their adult life. For example, it is presumed that a parent with an alcohol disease affects their children; therefore, the child is likely to be at risk of becoming an alcoholic or have characteristics of a child of an alcoholic). Their *soul pain* will continue to be unabated. *Soul pain* does not miss the opportunity to exact agony. If victimized children do not forgive and release their abuser, the imprint of abuse will remain indelible in their hearts and souls. The Bible says, "Why is my pain perpetual…" (Jeremiah 15:18). In the depths of *soul pain*, sufferers ask God this question every day.

These facts may be true for some people, but not for all people. However, generally speaking, living lives of abuse results in poisoned hearts which have difficulty forgiving, loving, or trusting self or others. *Soul pain* hardens the heart to the point of uselessness. Dread, sorrow, anxiety on account of *soul pain* overwhelms the heart. Unresolved *soul pain* remains in the heart and pleasure for the things of God cannot be found. The Bible says, "Beloved, do not think it strange concerning the fiery trial which is to try you, as though some strange thing happened to you" (1 Peter 4:12). Trials and tribulations will always occur throughout the lives of sufferers in some capacity, but it is the attitude of the heart that concerns Almighty God. Sufferers must trust God with all of their hearts—even when godly alternatives aren't apparent.

Transformed

Believers have a new intangible heart and out of the new heart, new thoughts flow. Only God has the power to transform deceitful hearts. Only God's redemptive love can change the hearts of His children. The root of a transformed heart is love, grace, and forgiveness. These divine gifts flow from God's heart to the heart of believers, which is transformed daily. These divine gifts flow out of transformed hearts to heal our souls. However, these gifts are not just for us, they are to be shared with others. Giving of oneself through unconditional love, grace, or forgiveness is unnatural to natural man, but unabashedly natural to believers. Through redemption, believers receive the essence of Almighty God. God gifts His children with Himself, His Son, and His Holy Spirit. Best yet, God is alive and living within the hearts of His children. For this reason, believers live with new purpose.

Unconditional love, grace, and forgiveness may not be easy for believers to offer in times of hurt, brokenness, and *soul pain*, but as the spiritual heart grows, greater are the gifts believers can bestow upon humanity. The Bible says, "A new commandment I give to you, that you love one another; as I have loved you, that you also love one another" (John 13:34). A new spiritual birth is the beginning of a new life with Almighty God. The intangible heart changes believers into new creations. At the second birth, the heart of a sinner is changed by God the Holy Spirit. We now have a new nature and can walk upright as loving children of the Almighty God.

It confounds the world when Christians with transformed hearts can love, give grace, and forgive people who have harmed them. It becomes a testimony when we who have overcome *soul pain,* use our *soul pain,* and our gifts from God to glorify Him on earth. God will take away the stubborn and rebellious heart that has been tainted by all kinds of wickedness and evil to give His children a clean transformed heart. A clean willing heart that is receptive to the things of God is His gift to us. The good news is that, through the efficacious blood of Christ, those who once suffered can be healed and set free from all past hurts.

Our greatest hurts can be our greatest testimony. God's love that overflows out of the Christian heart is joy in the Lord. The Bible says, "Be glad in the Lord, and rejoice, O righteous, and shout for joy, all you upright in heart!" (Psalm 32:11). Love covers all because Christian love is not a feeling. It is charity and mercy toward others that comes from a transformed heart. *Unconditional love is part of our spiritual DNA as believers.* This kind of love can only come from a clean heart that has been transformed by a mighty and holy God. Christian love is un-selfish and unconditional. The Bible says, "Create in me a clean heart, O God, and renew a right spirit within me" (Psalm 51:10). God the Holy Spirit gives the transformed heart the power to make the heart, pliable, open to love and immovable in Him.

God's grace given to the Christian through a transformed heart looks past the faults of others. The Bible says, "For the grace of God has appeared that offers salvation to all people" (Titus 2:11). Those who willingly give grace can testify about the glory of God and the love of Jesus Christ. Believers are encouraged to continue to live in grace through faith in Jesus Christ. Grace empowers us to love sinners because Jesus Christ loves them. *Grace is part of our spiritual DNA.*

God's forgiveness, given through a transformed heart, releases believers from the attachment to *soul pain*. Forgiveness frees us from bondage. Forgiveness gives us strength to love ourselves and love those who have harmed, disappointed, or betrayed us. Christians can forgive by faith in Jesus Christ because of our love and obedience to Him. The Bible says, "Be kind and compassionate to one another, forgiving each other, just as in Christ God forgave you" (Ephesians 4:32). The torment of *soul pain* can be better addressed with a transformed heart, if not remedied all together. *Forgiveness is part of the believer's spiritual DNA.*

All can be redeemed to Almighty God through faith in Jesus Christ. Jesus Christ is the world's redeemer. Many have accepted His invitation and there are many who will refuse. Jesus Christ is alive and always interceding on our behalf to our Heavenly Father. The Bible says, "I will give you a new heart and put a new spirit in you; I will remove from you your heart of stone and give you a heart of flesh" (Ezekiel 36:26). With a transformed heart, sufferers of *soul pain* can become free to love our family, friends, and the unlovable. The Christian must pray for those who harmed them and ask God to transform their hearts to have faith in His Son Jesus Christ, and to do good works in their lives.

The transformed heart allows God the Holy Spirit to lead, teach, and convict believers to have a biblical view of life. Christians' hearts are transformed, while God the Holy Spirit enables us to see life through righteous eyes. When we have a hurting heart because of *soul pain*, we must pray for healing for our broken heart. When bitterness creeps into our hearts, we must pray to be kind. When there is anger in our hearts, we must pray for love. When there is sin in our hearts, we must pray for forgiveness and repent. The Bible says, "Above all else, guard your heart, for everything you do flows from it" (Proverbs 4:23). A transformed heart becomes tender, moldable, and used by God through faith in His Son, Jesus Christ. It is the contrite heart that Almighty God wants, and it is the transformed heart that allows us to have true fellowship with Almighty God. Believers must surrender their hearts to Jesus Christ.

Chapter 28

A Transformed Mind

"Do not conform to the pattern of this world but be transformed by the renewing of your mind. Then you will be able to test and approve what God's will is—his good, pleasing and perfect will". (Romans 12:2)

ॐॐॐॐॐॐ

The Sufferer

Soul pain can sear the conscience causing sufferers to act upon, be satisfied with, or delight in sinful actions. *Soul pain* gnaws at the mind with worry, anxiety, and doubt leaving sufferers confused. When confusion sets in, the undisciplined mind is open for Satan to do what he does best in the world (steal, kill, destroy). Dishonest voices begin to exercise great influence and sufferers who listen to these voices become desensitized to what is right and godly. Bondage of the mind is more powerful than the imprisonment of the body. An undisciplined mind can project polluted thoughts. When those polluted thoughts are acted upon, they become sinful actions and negative behaviors. Those actions can leave a trail of unresolved hurt, pain, and destruction. Further, sufferers may interpret God's Word to mean something that is totally opposite of its true meaning. Such a compromise results in not having enough spiritual strength to stand against the winds of wickedness.

Sufferers who are seriously broken, have difficulty progressing past their hurt. They waste so much time on thoughts of how bad they feel that their lives become stuck at the point of their pain. Their viewpoint in life begins and ends at their hurt. As time goes on, they get older but, because of fear, sufferers may unwittingly not mature. They are fixated on avoidance and, to avoid being hurt again, they will do whatever is necessary to hinder or eliminate any further *soul pain*. Subsequently, sufferers cannot truly enjoy the abundant life Jesus Christ has promised. Sure, sufferers may function like happy people; however, spiritually they are sad. Memories of their pain is like a broken record constantly replaying in their minds.

Human beings have vulnerabilities that Satan will readily exploit. Sin still reigns, choices must be made, and the mind is the battlefield of spiritual warfare. Satan will constantly infiltrate as many minds as he can and take as many souls as possible to Hell with him. Satan has nothing to lose. *Soul pain* may momentarily stop sufferers from depending on or thinking Godly thoughts, but should the conscience of sufferers become obligated to Almighty God alone, there is hope. Satan has already been defeated by Jesus Christ.

Transformed

The root of a transformed mind is renewal. There is renewal in the way believers think. Gradually, what we once believed to be true by the world's standards is transformed by the absolute truth of God's Word. When believers become children of

God, we must be diligent in how and what we think. The Bible says, "Finally, brothers, whatever is true, whatever is honorable, whatever is just, whatever is pure, whatever is lovely, whatever is commendable, if there is any excellence, if there is anything worthy of praise, think about these things" (Philippians 4:8). God demands that Christians think true and pure things.

Joseph (the Patriarch in the Old Testament) was thrown into a well by his brothers, unjustly arrested for a crime he did not commit, and imprisoned for at least for two years. Joseph did not blame God for his circumstances, nor act upon any sinful thoughts. God blessed him for his faithfulness while he was in prison. He was placed as an overseer over the prisoners. After all he endured, Joseph saw God's hand in his life. God set into motion circumstances where Joseph would rule. When he was released from prison, he became second in command in Egypt. Joseph is a great example of someone having a transformed mind, set on Almighty God. The Bible says, "… demolish arguments and every pretension that sets itself up against the knowledge of God, and we take captive every thought to make it obedient to Christ" (2 Corinthians 10:5). Believers should be aware that we are not wise and need to humbly ask God to give us wisdom to make godly decisions. Believers need wisdom to think like Jesus Christ. We need wisdom to have a mind of faith for we can do nothing without Jesus Christ.

The mind is the invisible element of the brain that processes thoughts, feelings, behaviors, and memories. When believers try to live righteous lives in our own merit, we become short sighted of the things of heaven. We rely too heavily on our own will and intellect, which is limited to sheer human understanding. Spiritual thinking can only come from God the Holy Spirit. Believers should ask ourselves, "Are my spirit and thoughts aligned with the Word of God?" The Bible says, "For who knows a person's thoughts except their own spirit within them? In the same way no one knows the thoughts of God except the Spirit of God" (1 Corinthians 2:11). God alone knows the thoughts and spirit of man.

God the Holy Spirit will take hold of the transformed mind and give us a biblical perspective – a perspective of clarity in thought with biblical understanding. Thoughts are so commanding that they develop our character and, therefore, thoughts must be ruled by God the Holy Spirit. The Bible says, "The Lord—knows the thoughts of man…" (Psalm 94:11). When the sufferer is weak, Jesus Christ is our strong tower. Jesus Christ is our peace. Residing in His peace, we develop the ability to think right, reason right, make proper judgments, and do God's will. The believer's weapon against spiritual warfare is a clear mind full of God's truth. It is mighty and immensely powerful.

When in the pit of *soul pain*, we must fill our minds with things from above, and meditate on the Word of God. Believers are blessed with the treasured gift of the mind of Jesus Christ. Having the mind of Jesus Christ, we can have His thoughts, and His viewpoint in every circumstance through the power of God the Holy Spirit. *Soul pain* may come in many forms, but the transformed mind can handle any negative effects in ways that are implausible to man, but possible to Almighty God.

Believers should thank God every day for sound minds guided by God the Holy Spirit, so when believers are tested or tempted, we have enough wisdom to stand strong in the Lord and against the tactics of Satan. Believers are empowered to stop sin where it starts, in the mind. As we spiritually change, God the Holy Spirit will convict us to the point that the mere thought of ungodliness troubles our spirits. By renewing the spiritual mind, believers can have wisdom from God and the righteousness of Jesus Christ. The Bible says, "Consider what I say, and may the Lord give you understanding in all things" (2 Timothy 2:7). Don't act upon ungodly thoughts. Instead, surrender the mind to Jesus Christ.

Chapter 29

Rebuke the Victim Spirit

"Consider it pure joy, my brothers and sisters, whenever you face trials of many kinds, because you know that the testing of your faith produces perseverance".

(James 1:2-3)

ৡৡৡৡৡৡ

The Sufferer

Soul pain opens the door to victimization – the opportune condition for Satan and his minions to manipulate the spirit. In this condition, sufferers can know something is a lie and still give into Satan's illusion of pleasure. Sufferers remain captive when they don't give their *soul pain* to God. Instead, they live in it and the consequences of unaddressed *soul pain* (i.e., a hardened heart, a pierced soul, low self-esteem, and an impaired mind) remain. In this state, sufferers are dangerously wounded vessels. As the saying goes, "Hurt people ultimately hurt other people." Sufferers may not be able to conceptually understand the *soul pain* they have endured or are enduring and their inability to conceptualize it often leads to lives of chaos and stagnation. No fruitful quality of life can be produced only needless suffering. This describes the life in which the "victim spirit" has been released. The spirit takes up residence in the lives of sufferers and remains as long as sufferers continue to reside in valleys of hopelessness. That spirit can be with them all the days of their lives. The "victim spirit," must be broken because it brings no joy only heartache.

Soul pain associated with the "victim spirit" presents itself in many different areas in life with many symptomatic behaviors. Sufferers spend a lot of time focusing on the pain they feel instead of seeking solutions. Focusing on the pain elicits strong feelings of depression and sufferers feel they are only existing in life but cannot partake in the joys life has to offer. To family and friends, sufferers may appear to function normally in the world, but their hearts, minds, and souls experience turbulent spiritual warfare. Due to *soul pain*, they sometimes negatively identify themselves as: stupid, failures, unspiritual, the problem, etc. These labels are placed upon the sufferer themselves because of a "victim spirit."

Negative lifestyle choices can be symptoms of *soul pain* resulting in a "victim spirit." The Bible says, "Now the works of the flesh are evident: sexual immorality, impurity, sensuality, idolatry, sorcery, enmity, strife, jealousy, fits of anger, rivalries, dissensions, divisions, envy, drunkenness, orgies, and things like these. I warn you, as I warned you before, that those who do such things will not inherit the kingdom of God" (Galatians 5:19-21). Every believer desires to have a loving relationship with Almighty God, which is one of the great promises of Jesus Christ. However, life's trials, lifestyle choices, or a "victim spirit" can hinder that promise. To continue to live with a "victim spirit" is to satisfy corrupt sinful desires of the flesh. The Bible says, "For the mind that is set on the flesh is hostile to God, for it does not submit to God's law; indeed, it cannot" (Romans 8:7). To defeat the "victim spirit" is to live for God and be led by the Holy Spirit. Sufferers must choose how they want to live. The latter choice occurs in a loving relationship with Almighty God.

Transformed

Only Jesus Christ can close the door to *soul pain*. He is a shield for the hurting soul. The believing sufferer can stop living with a "victim spirit" and live a wonderful life with the Godhead. They start by asking, "God what are you showing me in this moment?" while trusting and believing God is in control. In their depression, believers can have abundant life knowing that God Almighty causes all things – even our *soul pain* – to work for our good. Therefore, we are never victims. Further, we must believe what Jesus Christ has promised us. The Bible says, "… I came that they may have life and have it abundantly" (John 10:10). Sufferers with a "victim spirit" focus on their pain and their hurt instead of the counsel of Jesus Christ. Conversely, the believer's identity is in their second birth where Jesus Christ reigns. There is no condemnation for the numerous sins believers committed or will commit. Jesus Christ offered Himself to be the Savior of the entire world and He offered Himself as the ultimate Sacrifice. He was both the offeror (gives the invitation of eternal life with Almighty God) and the offering (shed His blood on the cross so the world could be saved). He is the way to defeat the "victim spirit." The Bible says, "… Beloved, do not believe every spirit, but test the spirits to see whether they are from God" (1 John 4:1). The "victim spirit" is the impediment of freedom and liberty, but God's Word makes life worth living. His word ministers to the weak soul.

The Bible says, "Therefore if any man be in Christ, he is a new creature: old things are passed away; behold, all things are become new" (2 Corinthians 5:17). The heart is touched by the loving hand of Jesus Christ. The dead spirit is awakened by the power of the God the Holy Spirit. Finally, as His children, we take on the Spirit of the Almighty God leaving no room for a "victim spirit." The Bible says "It is the Spirit who gives life; the flesh is no help at all. The words that I have spoken to you are spirit and life" (John 6:63). Because of Jesus Christ, sufferers can walk in the newness of a righteous spirit. Sin no longer has dominion over believers. Through the Holy Spirit we escape the corrupted ways of the world. For these reasons, the children of God can live in peace, love, and joy. Not heartache, misery and *soul pain*. The hearts of believers have been transformed because they are the recipients of Jesus Christ's love and our past hurts can be used to glorify the Almighty God. Our past hurts no longer define who we are. The children of God receive new titles and new positions, which gives us power over the "victim spirit," sin, corruption, and hopelessness. Becoming children of God also guarantees that we will receive new titles and positions in the Kingdom of God. Below is a brief list of the wonderful tiles and positions held by the children of God:

1. An heir – "So you are no longer a slave, but God's child; and since you are his child, God has made you also an heir. (Galatians 4:7).

2. A child of God – "Behold what manner of love the Father has bestowed on us, that we should be called children of God!" (1 John 3:1)

3. A Gift – "Behold, children are a gift of the LORD......" (Psalm 127:3)

4. Child of the Most High – "I said, "You are gods, And all of you are children of the Most High" (Psalm 82:6)

5. Christians – "So for a whole year Barnabas and Saul met with the church and taught great numbers of people. The disciples were called Christians first at Antioch" (Acts 11:26)

6. Saint – "Paul, an apostle of Jesus Christ by the will of God, to the saints which are at Ephesus, and to the faithful in Christ Jesus:" (Ephesians 1:1)

7. The Elect - "Therefore, as the elect of God, holy and beloved, put on tender mercies, kindness, humility, meekness, longsuffering;" (Colossians 3:12)

8. An Ambassador – "We are therefore Christ's ambassadors, as though God were making his appeal through us" (2 Corinthians 5:20)

9. Abraham's Seed – "If you belong to Christ, then you are Abraham's seed..." (Galatians 3:29)

10. A Chosen People, A Royal Priesthood, God's Special Possession – "But you are a chosen people, a royal priesthood, a holy nation, God's special possession, that you may declare the praises of him who called you out of darkness into his wonderful light" (1 Peter 2:9)

11. Temple of the Holy Spirit – "Do you not know that your bodies are temples of the Holy Spirit. . ." (1 Corinthians 6:19)

12. Righteousness of God – "God made him who had no sin to be sin for us, so that in him we might become the righteousness of God" (2 Corinthians 5:21)

13. Head and not the tail – "The LORD will make you the head, not the tail. If you pay attention to the commands of the LORD your God. . ." (Deuteronomy 28:13)

We who contend with a "victim spirit" must take hold of who we *ARE* in Jesus Christ. We must walk in our beloved descriptive titles with confidence to invigorate our hearts, minds, and souls as we rejoice in our new nature. Instead of bemoaning hard times, we allow the circumstances of life to be pillars of godly victories. Instead of focusing on our deficiencies, we focus on who we are knowing God's presence is with us at all times. Resting upon the healing grace of God, believers use our *soul pain* to encourage and lift others out of the reach of the "victim spirit" and into the newness of life. We use the pain in life to glorify God by telling the world how God delivered us from our pain. The Bible says, "And call upon me in the day of trouble; I will deliver you, and you shall glorify me" (Psalm 50:15).

The "victim spirit" caused by *soul pain* is a spiritual phenomenon that must be treated and healed spiritually. The divine healing in my life was profound and because of my faith in Jesus Christ, I did not become a victim of my circumstances, or live with a "victim spirit." Instead, I became victorious. Looking back over my life, I can see that God was always with me. His divine providence over my life overruled the evil intentions of Satan and blessed me tremendously even in the times when I did not follow the teachings of Jesus Christ. I can relate to Job when God doubled his blessing. The Bible says, "After Job had prayed for his friends, the LORD restored his fortunes and gave him twice as much as he had before" (Job 42:10). God knows my short comings and yet he forgives me anyway. I want the things that I do in life to shine as a beacon of the goodness and grace of Jesus Christ. Refuse to have a "victim spirit." Don't walk as a victim, walk in victory.

Chapter 30

Connected to the Right Source

"For I am convinced that neither death nor life, neither angels nor demons, neither the present nor the future, nor any powers, neither height nor depth, nor anything else in all creation, will be able to separate us from the love of God that is in Christ Jesus our Lord". (Romans 8:38-39)

❧❧❧❧❧❧

The Sufferer

God allows mankind to make their own decisions through-out their journey in life. For some, life is a wonderfully pleasant journey. For some, their journey may be uncomfortable and filled with many difficulties. For some, their personality and reckless behavior create obstacles and oppositions in their lives. Unfortunately for others, life can be an awful nightmare where drama and trauma created by others seems to never end. A nightmarish season(s) of *soul pain* in life can be encountered from infancy through old age. Making right decisions while being subjected to *soul pain* is extremely important. These decisions can turn sufferers toward God, connecting them to Him for protection. Conversely, decisions can turn sufferers away from God, disconnecting them from walking by faith.

Human disconnection from God began with Adam in the Garden of Eden. The Bible says, "…So, the LORD God banished him (Adam) from the Garden of Eden to work the ground from which he had been taken" (Genesis 3:23). Adam and Eve disobeyed God and their relationship with God became broken. This is where generational disconnection began for humanity. This disconnection is still strong and thriving today. God never wanted to be disconnected from His children, but because of sin, disobedience, rebellion, and lawlessness have disconnected the world from God. Jesus Christ's death on the cross reconnected mankind to God, but some people intentionally disconnect because they are too busy for God or they want to go their own way.

While suffering, thinking clearly is difficult. Some sufferers use denial to soothe their *soul pain*. For some, *soul pain* becomes a normal part of their daily lives. Yet for others there are times in life when they plead to God for mercy or relief from their enemies. In the depth of *soul pain*, sufferers may think God does not hear their cries of pain. The truth is that focusing on pain is so distracting they cannot connect with a Holy God. Consequently, sufferers can lose heart or even become resentful believing that God is angry with them for what they have done, not done, or what has been done to them. The Bible says, "Why is my pain unending and my wound grievous and incurable? …" (Jeremiah 15:18). When God does not give an immediate answer or one that aligns with their understanding, sufferers often turn to sinful acts which only ensures they will remain disconnected from God Almighty. Disconnected from God, the only thing left to do is seek faux peace. However, the spiritual tug of war taking place within the soul makes even faux peace elusive. The instant pain relief they seek to satisfy the flesh doesn't exist. All they need can be found in a solid connection with Almighty God, but instead of being connected to God's righteousness, many sufferers choose rebellion. God the Holy Spirit and rebellion cannot dwell in the same heart. The following is an example what it is like to have the semblance of a connection, but not be changed:

Connected but Not Changed:

"This story illustrates a woman who had a small house on the seashore of Ireland at the turn of the twentieth century. She was quite wealthy, but also quite frugal. The people were surprised, when she decided to be among the first to have electricity in her home. Several weeks after the installation, a meter reader appeared at her door. He asked if her electricity was working well, and she assured him it was. "I'm wondering if you can explain something to me," he said. "Your meter shows scarcely any usage. Are you using your power?" "Certainly," she answered. "Each evening when the sun sets, I turn on my lights just long enough to light my candles; then I turn them off." She's tapped into the power but didn't use it. Her house is connected, but not changed. Don't we make the same mistake she did? We, too — our SOULS are saved, but our HEARTS are unchanged — are connected to (Jesus Christ), but not altered. Trusting in Jesus Christ for salvation, but resisting transformation. We occasionally flip the switch, but most of the time we settle for shadows. What would happen if we left the light on? What would happen if we not only flipped the switch, but lived in the light? What changes would occur if we set about the task of dwelling in the radiance of Jesus Christ" [3]

There are sufferers who believe. They have accepted the invitation of Jesus Christ for Him to become their Lord and Savior, but they are having a difficult time trusting Him enough to allow God the Holy Spirit to change their sinful heart and souls. Yes, it takes time for a heart to appreciate the promises of God, but what would happen if while in *soul pain* believing sufferers allowed the light of Jesus Christ to shine bright within and through them? Jesus Christ gives His precious children the gift to connect with His Father if they choose to do so.

Transformed

Gifts of Being Connected:

Being connected to Jesus Christ is a gift in itself. There are other divine gifts believers can enjoy:

*An Inseparable Fellowship with Almighty God

*An Inseparable fellowship with Jesus Christ

*An Inseparable fellowship with a Helper, God the Holy Spirit

*Healing power over the flesh

*Healing power over unbelief

*Healing power over sin

*Agape Love

*God's Grace

*God's Mercy

*God's Truth

*Hope

*Righteousness

*Eternal Life

*Unspeakable Joy

*Forgiveness

*Faith

*Heart of Flesh

*Self-Discipline

*Salvation

*Divine wisdom

*Spiritual Discernment

*Divine Peace

*A Sound Mind

*Fellowship with Believers

This brief list enumerates only a few of gifts and blessings God has in store for those who love Him. When believers live in the realm of our second birth, we have access to all of these gifts and more. These gifts are not only to benefit believers, but believers can share these gifts with others. Being connected to the right source is a life altering experience that transforms believers to beloved children of God. For only those who have faith in Jesus Christ will receive these gifts. The Bible says, "Yet to all who did receive him, to those who believed in his name, he gave the right to become children of God" (John 1:12). Being connected to the right source gives believers the right to be heirs to all that is good and right in Jesus Christ.

More than we realize, Almighty God and His Word are intertwined in all circumstances – even in *soul pain*. While seeking God and connecting to the right source, our relationship with Jesus Christ grows, our hearts are filled with love for God and for others. God lovingly enfolds the world in His arms every day waiting for anyone to respond to His invitation. He loves the people of the world regardless of our sinfulness. We need only to embrace God's love, forgiveness, grace, and mercy as loving gifts. God the Holy Spirit made these gifts available to fallen and frail humanity to connect with Almighty God. These gifts are free and accessible to assist all to become obedient children of God. Prayer is another way believers are connected to God. The Bible says, "In the same way, the Spirit helps us in our weakness. We do not know what we ought to pray for, but the Spirit himself intercedes for us through wordless groans" (Romans 8:26). Believers must be forever mindful that we are connected to God by the power of God the Holy Spirit.

In the Old Testament, once a year, the Levite Priest went into the Holy of Holies to atone for their sins and the sins of Israel. In the New Testament, Jesus Christ's death on the cross, atoned for the our sins and we are no longer separated from Almighty God. Believers have access to Almighty God and His mighty throne at any time because of the blood shed by Jesus Christ. The Bible says, "Therefore, brothers and sisters, since we have confidence to enter the Most Holy Place by the blood of Jesus" (Hebrews 10:19). Our souls are the most inner place within human body, and they belong to Jesus Christ. Being connected to Jesus Christ allows us to give our *soul pain*, and the burden associated with it, to Him. God the Holy Spirit reveals this work to believers so that we can genuinely appreciate all that Jesus Christ has done and will do in our lives. The Bible says, "Jesus Christ is the same yesterday and today and forever" (Hebrews 13:8). We do not know the wisdom of God nor all of the things He has prepared for His children, but God has been revealed through Jesus Christ and His power in believers' lives through God the Holy Spirit. The connection with God Almighty is a privilege and honor not a right and is granted to believers of Jesus Christ.

To be in God's presence, believers must slow down and set aside time to intentionally connect with Him. The Bible says, "…I will send to you from the Father—the Spirit of truth who goes out from the Father—he will testify about me" (John 15:26). In antiquity, God spoke to His people through His prophets. While Jesus Christ lived on earth, He revealed Heaven to the people. After Jesus Christ's death, God the Holy Spirit was sent to dwell in the hearts of all believers. God the Holy Spirit teaches believers the nature of a Holy God, truth of the Holy Scriptures, how to pray, how to connect to God, and to spiritually discern events in their lives. The Bible says, "However, as it is written: "What no eye has seen, what no ear has heard, and what no human mind has conceived – the things God has prepared for those who love him – these are the things God has revealed to us by his Spirit. The Spirit searches all things, even the deep things of God" (1 Corinthians 2:9-10). God the Holy Spirit is alive, exceedingly active in the life of every believer, and it is important for believers to acknowledge the spiritual part of their being. Their connection to Jesus Christ through God the Holy Spirit is crucial.

Believers can and should bear witness concerning our connection with Jesus Christ. By that connection, the darkness in our heart and minds has been overcome by the light of Jesus Christ. Jesus Christ is the true light of the world. The Bible says, "…we also glory in our sufferings, because we know that suffering produces perseverance; perseverance, character; and character, hope. And hope does not put us to shame, because God's love has been poured out into our hearts through the Holy Spirit, who has been given to us" (Romans 5:3-5).

Remember, trials work patience in God's children and God's grace produces good character through trials. It is the connection with a Holy God that makes overcoming *soul pain* possible and transforms us into useful vessels for good. It is because of the connection with Jesus Christ that we can withstand the horrid effects of *soul pain*. It is because of the connection that we can become ambassadors of Jesus Christ. It is by the connection with Jesus Christ that believers are transformed to holiness. It is the connection with God the Holy Spirit that renews the mind of a sinner to righteousness. Believers will always be connected to the right source because of our faith in Jesus Christ.

Believers, suffering or not, have dual citizenship. Being dual citizens does not take away pain or problems. There will always be *soul pain*, traumas, tears, and pain in this world. It is unfortunate that *soul pain* can do a lot of harm, but be encouraged, God's glory can be manifested even in *soul pain*. Believers are connected to the only true source of life. *Soul pain* will never win because there is always hope available through Jesus Christ.

Chapter 31

The Void Only Jesus Christ Can Fill

"Delight yourself in the LORD, and he will give you the desires of your heart. Commit your way to the LORD;

trust in him and he will do this".

(Psalms 37:4-5)

৵৵৵৵৵৵

The Sufferer

There is an innate spiritual void within every human soul. The heart and soul consistently crave something to fill that void, but it is not humanly possible to fill spiritual voids. God created the void within humanity to drive us toward seeking and worshiping Him specifically. From birth, humanity is self-seeking. Infants cry to get their needs met. Children and teenagers think the world revolves around them and their needs. Adults rebel against God to obtain their desires of worldly success, monetary fortune, and material possessions. The Bible says, "You have planted much, but harvested little. You eat, but never have enough. You drink, but never have your fill. You put on clothes, but are not warm.

You earn wages, only to put them in a purse with holes in it" (Haggai 1:6). This text teaches that humanity is never content. We can never have enough material goods; therefore, material possessions are inadequate. Further, the world suggests we seek peace or fulfillment by looking within ourselves to find satisfaction. However, when we look within ourselves, there is only emptiness. Satisfaction created by human means never guarantees peace or fulfillment. There is nothing humans can do or dream on their own that will fill the void within the human soul.

Abusers often attempt to fill that void with acts of wickedness motived by the need for control, greed, mental illness, pride, arrogance, selfishness, or misplaced anger. They may even inflict *soul pain* on others because they've experienced it themselves as a result of loss, illness, death of a love one, or a plethora of other varied reasons which cause unwavering sorrow. Whatever the reason, abusers often seem tormented by *soul pain*. This torment drives them to seek peace – even if their peace comes at the cost of another's *soul pain*. The unfortunate truth is the cycle often repeats as the abused seeks rest for their distressed soul. There is hope. Jesus Christ can fill the spiritual void for both the abuser and the abused.

In pain, some sufferers cannot hear God when He speaks. Instead, they look to satisfy the hunger in their souls by engaging in inappropriate activities. But the Bible teaches, "Blessed are those who hunger and thirst for righteousness, for they will be filled" (Matthew 5:6). If those who seek righteousness shall be filled, then those who pursue passions and desires of the flesh will continue to be unfulfilled. The world tells man to live life their way, with the prime mission of gaining ultimate sensual pleasure. This hedonistic lifestyle is the custom of the world. It promotes gaining as much pleasure and instant gratification for oneself without delay, but after the pleasure is achieved the heart and soul remain empty, and the spiritual void remains. The Bible says, "But each person is tempted when he is lured and enticed by his own desire. Then desire when it has conceived gives birth to sin, and sin when it is fully grown brings forth death" (James 1: 14-15). Man fills the void with self-indulgence, sinful acts, worldly devices, pride, or rebellion. All of these actions are transgressions against the will of God. Executing lust filled passion keeps sufferers in the valley of darkness, an empty spiritual void. Those with lost souls and deceitful hearts, the spiritual void will forever be a long festering abyss.

Yielding to lust filled passion is sin and it heightens self-ishness in people causing them to have little or no concern for others. This is what makes inflicting *soul pain* on another human being easy. The abuser has become hard-hearted. The Bible says, "…abstain from the passions of the flesh, which wage war against your soul" (1 Peter 2:11). Sadly, in this age of technology, lust filled passion can be seen in many ways and not all of it is sexual. Consider this: The world is comprised of many people not engaging in interpersonal relationships or human touch. Over time, the human touch has been converted from face-to-face interaction, to contact made through electronic devices such as cell phones, tablets, and computers. The Bible says, "Do not conform to the pattern of this world, but be transformed by the renewing of your mind…" (Romans 12:2). Lust filled passion can be created by overuse or misuse of these technologies. Phubbing, the lack of human interaction can leave the soul empty as sufferers forever search for something that is unreachable. *Soul pain* creates distance between mankind and between man and God. So much more time is focused on the use of the newest technology than on human relationships. The obsession of lust filled passion to acquire and use the newest technology, breaks the basic need for loving relationships. To fill this void in the soul, sufferers often go against God's will to fill their frantic bleakness. Remaining in this bleak state magnifies *soul pain* and the accompanying emptiness. It hinders sufferers from living lives of freedom and the cycle of emptiness never ends. There will always be a void in every created being and humanity will always seek to fill that void. The void will never be satisfied by earthly means.

Transformed

The void inside the human soul is created by God because of love and not punishment. It was designed for us to see our need for God and to draw us closer to Him. Consequently, the void in every soul can only be filled to capacity by Jesus Christ. Only He can completely and sufficiently satisfy the emptiness within. He wants to fill the spiritual void that dwells in every soul with God the Holy Spirit. Through Jesus Christ, Almighty God fills the soul until it overflows. Therefore, while He provides for and protects His creation He also provides eternal life to His children. He knows who we will become through our relationship with Him; therefore, it is Jesus Christ who can make believers acceptable for God's kingdom.

Human beings are created in God's image, but in filling the void, the mind must be focused on righteousness and holiness through faith in Jesus Christ. The believer's heart, mind, and soul must become completely empty of self in order for Almighty God to fill the void with His love. The Bible says, "Therefore, if anyone is in Christ, the new creation has come: The old has gone, the new is here!" (2 Corinthians 5:17). As new creations, we begin to live under new rules, new knowledge, and a new direction in life. Jesus Christ becomes the center of our lives and lovingly our character and conduct change to please God.

The Bible says, "You were taught, with regard to your former way of life, to put off your old self, which is being corrupted by its deceitful desires; to be made new in the attitude of your minds; and to put on the new self, created to be like God in true righteousness and holiness" (Ephesians 4:22-24). When the void is filled, the desire to relieve *soul pain* with ungodly choices, are challenged with a desire to apply God's Word in life. The soul that is filled with God's love, forever seeks God's truth. The Bible says, "My soul thirsts for God, for the living God..." (Psalm 42:2). There is no joy greater than the joy of knowing and living for Almighty God.

Passion for the eternal accompanies a desire to earnestly trust Jesus Christ and seek the things of heaven. This type of passion is created when the desire to please God is more important than the desire to please self. Faith in Jesus Christ fills the void with unbridled joy, freedom from bondage, and new-found liberty. The Bible says, "You, my brothers and sisters, were called to be free. But do not use your freedom to indulge the flesh; rather, serve one another humbly in love" (Galatians 5:13). Affection for the eternally fulfilled passion pleases God. Jesus Christ fills the void to make us spiritually whole and complete. God the Holy Spirit brings freedom and power over sin. With the veil of darkness pulled back, the light of Jesus Christ shines bright, and believers become one with Jesus Christ. Our oneness with Him transforms us into shining lights illuminating this dark world.

The believer is blessed to have the void filled with God's agape love. Jesus Christ fills the void in the soul with peace, love, compassion, and godly wisdom. When the human heart opens up to receive the Lord, a spiritual new awakening arises within the soul. The spiritual awakening allows us to delight in the things of God even while in *soul pain*. The Bible says, "Likewise you also, reckon yourselves to be dead indeed to sin, but alive to God in Christ Jesus our Lord" (Romans 6:11).

The Lord earnestly fills the void in the new believer, spiritually weak, or the suffering believer because of *soul pain*. Jesus Christ filled the void in my tormented soul, while God drew me to Himself. God lovingly drew me into His kingdom before I knew what was happening. When I was young, I had a desire to be kind like my grandmother and began to love Jesus Christ with all my heart. While I was experiencing *soul pain*, I desired to have the right standing before Almighty God. I desire to share God's love, mercy, forgiveness, and grace with others as I travel through this life. Joy and happiness replaced heartache and misery in the void of my soul.

God the Holy Spirit continues to instruct believers in the ways of righteousness and brings believers into intimate relationship with Abba, Our Father. Through this relationship, the void we once had is continually filled until it overflows by Jesus Christ. Jesus Christ is our void filler, life stabilizer, and soul restorer.

Chapter 32

Jesus Christ The Mediator and Protector, He Is The Way

"Jesus said to him, "I am the way and the truth and the life. No one comes to the Father except through me". (John 14:6)

৵৵৵৵৵৵

Mediator

God designed a perfect plan of salvation to bring humanity to Himself through His Son, Jesus Christ. Jesus Christ's mission was preordained before the formation of the earth just as God preordained the life of every person before we are formed in our mothers' wombs. The Bible says, "The Lord has made everything for its purpose..." (Proverbs 16:4). Because He knows our purpose, Jesus Christ is the believers' answer to everything in life especially *soul pain*. He is the only answer to relieve it, remove it, and replace it with spiritual peace. The Bible says, "You are a hiding place for me; you preserve me from trouble; you surround me with shouts of deliverance" (Psalm 32:7). Jesus Christ loves and is faithful to His children to the utmost. He is our shelter in the time of storms.

The Bible foretold the coming of Jesus Christ in the Old Testament and the details of His life while on earth can be found in the New Testament. God's Son became human to become an example of how to have a relationship with Almighty God. He shed His blood as ransom on the cross for all. The Bible says, "For there is one God and one mediator between God and mankind, the man Christ Jesus" (1 Timothy 2:5). He is the Bread of Life, the Way, Good Sheppard, Emmanuel, Mediator, Redeemer, Resurrection of Life, and so much more. Jesus Christ is God's Word come to life and our Mediator in Heaven. He saves all from the penalty of sin and makes peace with God.

Jesus Christ left the holy and glorious place of heaven to take on a human nature for the world to be saved. Jesus Christ was clothed in humanity with an earthly body. Jesus Christ became the propitiation for God's wrath. He was the God Man (fully God and fully man), second in the Godhead. Jesus Christ diligently prepares the way for sinful men to be made spiritually whole. From the time of Jesus Christ's birth until He gave up His life on the cross at Calvary, Jesus Christ was God living in a blind world. Through His teaching, preaching, and healing, He showed the world the living God, the real, true, and unequivocal Almighty God. The Bible says, "And the Word became flesh and dwelt among us, and we have seen his glory, glory as of the only Son from the Father, full of grace and truth" (John 1:14). Jesus Christ, our Savior supplies His children with the power of God the Holy Spirit to overcome *soul pain*, heartache, and bitterness.

Jesus Christ, the Mediator speaks to the Father on behalf of His beloved believers throughout eternity. He mediates our hopes, dreams, desires, choices, sins, strengths, weaknesses, and *soul pain*. He loved humanity while He was in heaven with His Father, before He was sent to earth; He loved humanity while He walked the earth; He loved humanity while He was on the cross; He loves humanity today; and He will love humanity always and forever. The Bible says, ". . . the name of our Lord Jesus may be glorified in you, and you in him, according to the grace of our God and the Lord Jesus Christ" (2 Thessalonians 1:12). Believers are not to take Jesus Christ for granted. Just as God sets the righteous apart as His own, believers must set Jesus Christ apart as our own gracious Savior. The Bible says, "Know that the LORD has set apart his faithful servant for himself..." (Psalm 4:3). God calls the righteous unto Himself. We are chosen by God through His grace and are set apart for His pleasure.

Questions are often raised concerning Jesus Christ's deity. *How does Jesus Christ have power over sin, soul pain, and nature? How can Jesus Christ be God and man? Is Jesus Christ the only Son of God? Is Jesus Christ the only way to God? How can Jesus Christ save a sinner? How can Jesus Christ be the believer's Mediator?* These questions cannot be answered with a simple "yes" or "no". These questions can be eloquently answered by the many different biblical scholars of our time, but the answers can only be believed by faith. By faith we believe that Jesus Christ lived a sinless life among humanity. By faith we believe He lived a life of service to all people. By faith we believe He is incarnate, Emanuel, God with us. By faith we believe The Son now sits at the right hand of God as our Mediator to reconcile His children to God and as an Intercessor in order for His children to have the right standing before a righteous and Holy God. The Bible says, "And God placed all things under his feet and appointed him to be head over everything for the church, which is his body, the fullness of him who fills everything in every way" (Ephesians 1:22-23).

The Protector

Believers who have endured painful occurrences in life need Jesus Christ to help us defeat our *soul pain*. He protects believers from the long-lasting effects of *soul pain*. He protects us from Satan, his minions, and gives wisdom to discern the cunning strategies of the adversary. *Soul pain* induced by self or by others can cause the human soul to feel weak, but through the grace of Jesus Christ, we have the ability to endure impossible events in life if we choose. When evil feelings, thoughts, voices, or emotions recur in the mind, believers endure by not entertaining ungodliness at any time because we know ungodly behavior does not heal *soul pain*. Instead, we rely on the ever-present help of Jesus Christ, our protector. Sadly, even believers can be crippled by the effects of *soul pain*, but thankfully Jesus Christ is willing to erase the pain if we allow Him to do so. The Bible says, "The Lord is my strength and my song, and he has become my salvation; this is my God, and I will praise him, my father's God, and I will exalt him" (Exodus 15:2). Jesus Christ bestows mercy on His children when we are at our weakest. His grace is magnified in believers when we feel powerless.

Jesus Christ is our Protector from the world's untruths and the pandemonium in the land. Jesus Christ understands *soul pain*, suffering, and burdens in life because while on earth, His life included these things. The help Jesus Christ offers is not limited by our specific location. His help can be found in the most remote corners of the earth and bring healing wherever it may be needed. There is nowhere to hide from Him. The Bible says, "For nothing is hidden except to be made manifest; nor is anything secret except to come to light" (Mark 4:22).

Some specific *soul pain* is a byproduct of sin. Jesus Christ is sufficient to combat all *soul pain* and is the answer to all of life's challenges. Jesus Christ protects His loved ones from the mayhem of life and consoles us through our troubles while God the Holy Spirit keeps us from sinning. This means that through Him our heartache is relieved from the misery of this fallen world. Jesus Christ came to triumph over wickedness in the world, set the captives free, and destroy the works of the devil. Therefore, Jesus Christ's work on the cross defends us when weakened by our enemies or the pressures of the world. He gives us hope when hope cannot be imagined. Jesus Christ is the Good News the world seeks.

Soul pain disables the will of man, but because of love, Jesus Christ makes our lives, problems, heartaches, and *soul pain* His own. He can handle it all because Jesus Christ is blessed with all power. The Bible says, "For in him all things were created: things in heaven and on earth, visible and invisible, whether thrones or powers or rulers or authorities; all things have been created through him and for him" (Colossians 1:16).

From the beginning, and throughout Scripture Jesus Christ is the Protector of mankind. The Bible says, "You, however, are not in the realm of the flesh but are in the realm of the Spirit, if indeed the Spirit of God lives in you. And if anyone does not have the Spirit of Christ, they do not belong to Christ" (Romans 8:9). Believers are always to trust God the Father, God the Son, and God the Holy Spirit. Look unto the suffering Savior and praying with faith, not to be delivered into the hands of our enemy (Satan) because of *soul pain*. The Bible says, "The LORD will fight for you; you need only to be still" (Exodus 14:14). Jesus Christ is the Resurrection and the Life. He redeems and resurrects lost and dead souls every day. Jesus Christ is the only Protector of the human soul.

The Way

Jesus Christ is the only Way to the Father in heaven. He is the true gift that keeps on giving. *Soul pain* causes serious life situations that only Jesus Christ, the Mediator, Protector, and the Way can answer. The heartache of *soul pain* hinders the soul and mind from being comforted. We seek Jesus Christ to straighten the brokenness in the human soul because only He can answer our prayers, especially those related to *soul pain.*

Dear Lord Jesus Christ please relieve my *soul pain.* I need your help:

1. When I am in despair and I don't trust because people who are supposed to love me have harmed me. (Unforgiveness)

2. When life is so painful, and I am contemplating suicide. (Hopelessness)

3. When I look into a mirror and don't like what I see, and it shakes me to the core. (Spiritual Brokenness)

4. When my image of God reflected in the mirror does not line up with my DNA. (Spiritual Warfare)

5. To stop putting catastrophic substances in my body (Temple of the Holy Spirit) that will harm me. (Lust of the Flesh)

6. To believe my body is not my own and when I express to the world that this is my body to choose what I want to do with it. (Pride)

7. When I desire to be under the sheets with someone other than my spouse. (Lust of the Flesh)

8. To be kind instead of unloving and bitter toward my family, friends, or strangers. (Resentfulness)

9. To have peace and strength in my soul when I am behind prison walls. (Hopelessness)

10. To acknowledge that I am an abuser and I need to change my life to please God. (Rebellion)

11. To have a kind and compassionate heart because of abuse. (Mercilessness)

12. When I am ready to give up on my marriage. (Helplessness)

13. When I have sexual desires that do not line up with God's Word. (Lust of the Flesh)

14. When I think about killing the life growing inside of me. (Disobedient)

15. When I think about taking the life of another. (Lawlessness)

16. When I am running from God. (Faithlessness)

17. To be sensitive to God the Holy Spirit when He is speaking to me and I am too rebellious to listen. (Rebellious)

18. To be the Christian you desire me to be. (Faithfulness)

Sin is manifested in many ways, but Jesus Christ is the giver of truth, true life, true peace, true delight, and true gladness. He cleanses all unrighteousness within the hearts of mankind to make us spiritually whole. The Bible says, "My God, my rock, in whom I take refuge, my shield, and the horn of my salvation, my stronghold and my refuge, my savior; you save me from violence. I call upon the Lord, who is worthy to be praised, and I am saved from my enemies" (2 Samuel 22:3-4). An intimate relationship with God was started in the Garden of Eden and God still desires to maintain intimate relationships with His children today and throughout eternity. Mankind is helplessly and hopelessly unable to please God, heal *soul pain*, or save our souls for heaven by any human means. The Bible says, "And I will put enmity between you and the woman, and between your seed and her Seed (the Savior); He shall bruise your head, and you shall bruise His heel." (Genesis 3:15). This Seed (Jesus Christ) will crush the head of Satan which was promised by God. Jesus Christ is the way the world can have free access to Almighty God.

Jesus Christ is an exemplary example for His church. He sought direction from His Heavenly Father before He made any decision, He obeyed His Father's every commandment without complaining to His Father regarding His death. When believers suffer from spiritual *soul pain,* it is difficult for us not to complain. When sinful thoughts begin to invade our minds, instead of complaining we should search God's Word for direction and listen to God the Holy Spirit for guidance. Jesus Christ is the Way to crush strongholds in our lives. Jesus Christ is the Way to live a righteous life here on earth. Jesus Christ is the Way out of *soul pain*. Jesus Christ is the Mediator, Protector, and Guardian for His children. Jesus Christ is the only Way to eternal life.

Chapter 33

The Word of God "Brings Forth Life Not Heartache"

"Your word is a lamp for my feet, a light on my path".

(Psalm 119:105)

ॐ ॐ ॐ ॐ ॐ ॐ

The Sufferer

The Holy Bible is not a book of myths or the product of someone's vivid imagination. It's not a book full of fairytales, superstitions, or demands. The Holy Bible is God's Word (Logos), which is powerful and active in the lives of His children and the world. The Holy Bible is the absolute truth. It is the truth of the universe. The Bible says, "The entirety of Your word is truth, And every one of Your righteous judgments endures forever" (Psalm 119:160). The Holy Bible is God speaking to the physical world about Himself, His precious Son, and His love for all He creates.

False teachers' discourse of lies can distort God's Word. In so doing, they profess their own words as the truth, deceiving the vulnerable by their words and deeds while leading those with *soul pain* to a deeper sense of separation and brokenness. The Bible says, "If anyone teaches a different doctrine and does not agree with the sound words of our Lord Jesus Christ and the teaching that accords with godliness, he is puffed up with conceit and understands nothing...." (1 Timothy 6:3-4).

Devastating *soul pain* can blind sufferers to the cure written in God's Word. *Soul pain* is a culprit of disbelief, doubt, and misery. When in *soul pain,* God's Word may not appear to be alive or active to sufferers. In fact, the Word of God may seem to be powerless words written on paper. The anguish of *soul pain* can make sufferers flail about in the wilderness of society instead of seeking God's Word to help remove an unauthorized enemy within the soul. Many times, sufferers may be too spiritually weak to even try to do what's right. *Soul pain* has a consuming presence in the lives of sufferers, which may prompt them to compromise their soul because of fear, or willfully refuse to obey the Word of God out of rebellion.

The Bible says, "In fact, everyone who wants to live a godly life in Christ Jesus will be persecuted," (2 Timothy 3:12). Therefore, having steadfast confidence in God's Word is essential while ignoring God's Word is damaging. Sinning to relieve *soul pain* is a terrible option. Sin deceives and the cost of unrighteousness is not worth the heartache it causes. Believers are to receive, have faith in, and trust God's Word without hesitation or doubt because the Holy Scriptures are God speaking the absolute truth to the soul. There are many who will never believe that God's Word is true. Religion News states that:

"Most Americans believe, but not always in the
God of the Bible. To be sure, a majority, if a slim
one — 56 percent — say they believe in the con-
ventional all-loving, all-knowing, all-powerful God
of the Bible. The survey also showed that: Belief
in the God of the Bible declines with age. Those
under age 50 viewed God as less powerful and less
involved in earthly affairs than do older Americans.
Among college graduates, only 45 percent believe
in the God of the Bible. Views of God also tend to
differ by political party and race. Seventy percent
of Republicans believe in the God of the Bible,
while only 45 percent of Democrats do. But among
Democrats, there are big differences in views of
God when it comes to race; 70 percent of non-white
Democrats believe in the God of the Bible — com-
parable to the rate among Republicans. Then there
are the hardcore disbelievers: about 10 percent
who say they don't believe in the God of the Bible
or a higher power." [4]

When God's Word has no place in the heart of man, long-term spiritual misery becomes a part of life. *Soul pain* thrives and survives. The divine power of God's conversion of the heart is not appreciated. When the divinity of Jesus Christ expressed in the Holy Word is repudiated, darkness in the corrupted heart allows sin to abide allowing *soul pain* to prevail. When God's Word is not adhered to, His voice is ignored or disobeyed, the power of God the Holy Spirit is neglected, the magnificent works of Jesus Christ are rejected. When decisions are made to go our own way, we should expect condemnation, judgement, and for the creation to not experience wholeness. The Bible says, "But if you will not obey the voice of the Lord, but rebel against the commandment of the Lord, then the hand of the Lord will be against you…" (1 Samuel 12:15). When pride and wickedness, fills the heart, there is no room for God's Word to abide. When problems in life are unending and solutions are not found, it is hard for sufferers to understand the spiritual peace that only comes to those who believe. As stated earlier, when the heart is full of *soul pain*, heartache, and misery, sufferers may abuse innocent victims, divulge in negative habits/behaviors, or self-harm themselves all in an effort to find some relief. God's Word is needed to understand and fight against the spiritual warfare of *soul pain*. When God's Word abides in the soul, it crushes all ungodliness. The world only believes and is satisfied with what is seen, but the Holy Scriptures commands believers to focus on what is not seen. No victory over *soul pain* or true elimination of it will happen if there is doubt regarding God's Word.

Transformed

The Bible says, "In the beginning was the Word, and the Word was with God, and the Word was God. He was with God in the beginning. Through him all things were made; without him nothing was made that has been made. In him was life, and that life was the light of all mankind" (John 1:1-4). Jesus Christ, the Word of God, revealed the mind and heart of God to the world. The Word was with God and the Word of God is truth. The Word of God is eternal. There are no adverse reactions associated with using the Word of God. In fact, God's Word is the standard by which societies and personal determinations were measured. God's Holy Scriptures are powerful words that calm the soul. The Bible says, "Every word of God proves true; he is a shield to those who take refuge in him" (Proverbs 30:5). The Bible is profitable, it expresses the nature, character, and attributes of Almighty God. The purpose of life can be found in God's Word. It teaches God's children how to live faithfully. For issues not found in God's Holy Word, believers have a Father we can pray to for an answers and direction. God's Word gives hope, heals, restores, and revives. Hope is always accessible in the Word of Almighty God. Hope is knowing that there will always be an effectual change within the heart of believers in this life and the life hereafter. *Soul pain* can be defeated if we allow God's Word to manifest in our minds, bodies, and souls. God's Word is food for the soul that should be consumed daily. God's Holy Scriptures offer transformation when His children suffer with *soul pain*. God's Word is sweet medicine needed for the tormented soul and the deceitful heart.

God's Word:

1. Heals - He sent his word, and healed them, … (Psalm 107:20)

2. Restores - But I will restore you to health and heal your wounds,' declares the LORD. (Jeremiah 30:17)

3. Gives Power - So faith comes from hearing, and hearing through the word of Christ. (Romans 10:17)

4. Requires Obedience - He replied, "Blessed rather are those who hear the word of God and obey it." (Luke 11:28)

5. Endures Forever - Heaven and earth will pass away, but my words will never pass away. (Matthew 24:35)

6. Is Flawless - As for God, his way is perfect: The Lord's word is flawless; he shields all who take refuge in him. (Psalm 18:30)

7. Is the Absolute Truth - For the word of the Lord is right and true; he is faithful in all he does. (Psalm 33:4)

8. Gives Strength – I can do all things through him who strengthens me. (Philippians 4:13)

9. Cleanses – You are already clean because of the word I have spoken to you. (John 15:3)

10. Gives Hope – but those who hope in the LORD will renew their strength. They will soar on wings like eagles; they will run and not grow weary; they will walk and not be faint. (Isaiah 40:31)

God's Word illustrates spiritual power and how the believer can access that power. The Bible says, "This is the meaning of the parable: The seed is the word of God" (Luke 8:11). God's Word is seed planted in the heart that grows like a tree, immovable, and bearing good fruit. These seeds are rooted in Jesus Christ as the authority of life. The power of God's Word is flawless, it refreshes the soul, and makes the broken spirit whole. God's Word gives believers wisdom to discern corruption and wade through deception that parade as truth. The Bible says, "Therefore everyone who hears these words of mine and puts them into practice is like a wise man who built his house on the rock." (Matthew 7:24). God's Word restores the helpless soul. God's Word fills the gnawing pit in the soul where *soul pain* reigns. Where there is confusion, God's Word brings clarity. Where there is heartache, God's Word brings joy. Where there is strife, God's Word brings harmony. Where there is unforgiveness, God's Word brings compassion.

God's Word heals the brokenness between God and man. The Bible says, "Sanctify them in the truth; your word is truth" (John

17:17). God's Word tells the truth about Almighty God, His love, and His Heavenly Kingdom. God's Word tells the truth about redemption and salvation in Jesus Christ. God's Word tells the truth about humanity and its disjointedness. God's Word brings forth life and will never bring heartache. God's Word is essential to our existence just as the blood that flows in our veins.

Every Word of God's Holy Scripture is the absolute truth. God's Word is the guide for reason, spiritual wisdom and a manual of how to live a righteous life in this world. The only thing that lasts from generation to generation is God's Word. It never tears down, only lifts up. All ills, heartache, *soul pain*, and destruction in this world can be cured by the Word of God. The treasure of God's Word has been available before the foundation of the world and is always free to anyone who seeks the absolute truth. God's Word is Jesus Christ Incarnate.

Chapter 34

Lover of Our Soul

"Behold, all souls are mine". (Ezekiel 18:4)

❧❧❧❧❧❧

The Lost Soul

The original condition of every human soul is lost, a consequence inherited by humanity because of Adam's disobedience in Eden. Adam's sin created physical death and spiritual corruption, both characteristics of lost souls. ALL of Adam's descendants, throughout every generation, are penalized because of his sin. The lost soul is desolate, dismayed, dejected, and will never have peace because a lost soul is eternally separated from Almighty God. The Bible says, "… No one is good—except God" (Mark 10:18). Everyone has the same problem: man is lost because of sin and is due judgement. When the soul is lost, *soul pain* haunts the soul in ways that are unexplainable and Almighty God is not considered part of the equation as a resolution. The condition to correct the problem: confession of faith in Jesus Christ. God will not grant His promise if the condition is not met resulting in eternal damnation. However, the privilege of every believer is the promise: eternal life with Almighty God.

Man puts a price on their soul. They will strive for anything to quench the lust of the flesh. Those with lost souls do not spend time with God, meditate on the Holy Word, nor are they concerned with the health of their soul because they don't believe in the Son. The lost soul seeks worldly possessions, money, vile pleasure, fame, and lustful sin to fill the void. The Bible says, "We all, like sheep, have gone astray, each of us has turned to our own way..." (Isaiah 53:6). The lost soul will never have the right relationship with Almighty God, God the Son, and God the Holy Spirit because of their choice to reject Jesus Christ. The lost soul will remain in eternal darkness forever separated from Almighty God. Sacrificing a right relationship with Almighty God for worldly gain is the embodiment of idiocy.

People diligently embrace improving their physical bodies. The physique is groomed, shaped, and pampered all to obtain the admiration of the world. However, people don't diligently nourish the health of their souls which have a future with God in heaven. People intentionally forfeit feeding their souls in exchange for worldly possessions. This lack of nourishing spiritual health did not just begin. In antiquity, men of that time desired worldly fame and ignored the things of God. Instead of giving their souls to God, they sacrificed their souls for selfish egotistical pride. Absalom rebelled against his father David, had his brother killed, and never sat on the throne. His life ended tragically. He was the master of his own lost soul. Saul followed his pride/ego and disobeyed God. His life ended in suicide. He was the master of his own lost soul. Judas, a disciple of Jesus Christ betrayed His master for a few pieces of silver. His life ended in suicide. He was the master of his own lost soul. All three men thought their way was right, yet they lost everything. The Bible says, "What good is it for someone to gain the whole world, yet forfeit their soul?" (Mark 8:36). Human nature instinctively yields to its wants and desires. In doing so, lost souls are headed for destruction. The Bible says, "Yet there are some of you who do not believe. For Jesus had known from the beginning which of them did not believe …" (John 6:64). Willfully plunging into sin and wickedness gives way to short lived happiness and satisfaction. Sin hardens the heart and ruins the soul.

The lost soul is never satisfied. It is always seeking, searching, and never spiritually content. There are many people with lost souls who appear happy, but they don't know that their lost souls cannot be woven together by the Godhead because their lost souls are not saved without Jesus Christ. The lost soul is forever squandered without the Savior. Those with lost souls, sin without regret. The Bible says, "Whoever believes and is baptized will be saved, but whoever does not believe will be condemned" (Mark 16:16). God does not want anyone to depart from Him; however, lost souls can only be redeemed through Jesus Christ. God created many things in this world for His children to enjoy, but unfortunately humanity uses God's gifts to abuse and create havoc upon the lost souls.

The Shattered Lost Soul

Soul pain, heartache, and misery shatters the vulnerable soul. Shattered lost souls are in utter wretchedness because of *soul pain* or other circumstances that break the will of lost souls. The Bible says, "But your iniquities have made a separation between you and your God, and your sins have hidden his face from you so that he does not hear" (Isaiah 59:2). In the lives of shattered lost souls, *soul pain* goes deeper than unhappiness or heartache.

Shattered lost souls are in a human condition which stands in combative opposition to the joy only Jesus Christ can bring. Shattered lost souls suffer to the point of continual heartache. The condition of their souls promotes fear, despair, hopelessness, loneliness and so much more. Without God, there is incessant chaos, a hardened heart, and a worried mind found within them. The Bible says, "Take my yoke upon you, and learn from me, for I am gentle and lowly in heart, and you will find rest for your souls" (Matthew 11:29). Shattered lost souls will never find true rest on their own because they are engulfed by a multitude of uncertainty. Though Jesus Christ is their answer, shattered lost souls cannot hear the voice of God because they reject: Him, His Son, His Spirit, and His Word. This rejection separates them from the very thing they seek. The Bible says, "I will refresh the weary and satisfy the faint" (Jeremiah 31:25). Only God can satisfy shattered lost souls, but they desire things of the world. Shattered lost souls look for comfort in ungodliness and ungodliness can never solve their depraved spiritual condition. The Bible says, "Do not love the world or the things in the world. If anyone loves the world, the love of the Father is not in him" (1 John 2:15). Sin exacerbates the sordid condition and *soul pain* they experience. Regrettably, humanity uses God's created things to sin instead of to see God. If they would merely observe God's creation, he would reveal Himself in this world for His created beings to enjoy and be drawn to Him. Unfortunately, humanity uses God's gifts to abuse and create havoc upon shattered lost souls.

The Shattered Saved Soul

Faith in Jesus Christ saves souls from the penalty of sin and separation from Almighty God. Life can bring souls much joy or much pain. Souls can be saved, but even saved souls are not immune from *soul pain*, heartache, or suffering. Saved souls can be shattered, but shattered saved souls have hope based in their personal relationships with Jesus Christ. Saved souls can be shattered into many pieces because of spiritual pain rooted in numerous causes. Almighty God's children can suffer physical calamities, troubles, and spiritual spears from the adversary. Shattered saved souls can either turn to God to ease the pain or they may even turn from God while in the valley of despair. The choice to turn away from God will prolong their time in the depths of *soul pain*. But those souls who turn to their Heavenly Father are tenderly woven back together by the love of Jesus Christ. The shattered saved soul can always find comfort through their Lord and Savior Jesus Christ. We can turn to Jesus Christ to find peace to quiet the rumbling of our shattered saved souls. The Bible says, "…Praise the Lord, my soul; all my inmost being, praise his holy name. Praise the Lord, my soul, and forget not all his benefits; who forgives all your sins and heals all your diseases, who redeems your life from the pit and crowns you with love and compassion, who satisfies your desires with good things so that your youth is renewed like the eagle's" (Psalm 103:1-5).

Oh, how shattered saved souls desire to be held in the loving arms of Almighty God to receive His peace, joy and healing amid chaos. While our minds and emotions are engrossed in the ravages of *soul pain*, simultaneously shattered saved souls receive the favor of God. Jesus Christ heals all our infirmities, forgives all our sins, and grants us protection. The Bible says, "He restores my soul. He leads me in paths of righteousness for his name's sake" (Psalm 23:3). The Father rejuvenates shattered saved souls and restores us to fullness.

Only Jesus Christ heals the distraught shattered saved soul by bringing harmony, joy, freedom, happiness, and love into our lives. When shattered saved souls feel hopeless or helpless, God the Holy Spirit is always close by to move us toward spiritual healing. The spirit of God within shattered saved souls will not allow the heart, mind or body to give up on life because of *soul pain*. Though shattered, the saved soul can always draw near to what is good and right. Jesus Christ does not want His children to fall out of fellowship with His Father. He does not want His children to have shattered saved souls, but when saved souls are shattered, it is Jesus Christ's opportunity to heal us with His gospel.

Almighty God Is The Lover of Our Soul

The Bible says, "Then the LORD God formed a man from the dust of the ground and breathed into his nostrils the breath of life, and the man became a living being" (Genesis 2:7). God loves humanity more than we will ever know. Every soul is important to Him. Having an intimate relationship with Almighty God cannot be compared to any other relationship in the entire world. He loves all people despite our misbehavior, and He continually loves us no matter how many mistakes we make in life. God alone creates the soul of man. God is the creator of the cycle of life, He knows everyone's innermost parts, and the depths of every soul. He does not love based on what believers think, say, or do. He loves because that's who He is. The Bible says, "Whoever does not love does not know God, because God is love" (1 John 4:7). What a blessing it is to know that we have a loving God whose love never dies. The physical body can be seen by the human eye, which houses the soul. The soul is not made like the body which is mortal and fading every day. The soul lives for eternity either with God or without Him. Each soul is exceptionally created as a precious jewel and a treasured handiwork of Almighty God. The Bible says, "The Spirit of God has made me, and the breath of the Almighty gives me life" (Job 33:4). How wonderful it is to have a soul come to life and be able to live with a Holy God forever.

George Macdonald, in 1892 said *"Never tell a child,"* you *have a soul. Teach him, you are a soul; you have a body. As we learn to think of things always in this order, that the body is but the temporary clothing of the soul…"* [6]

Soul pain may cause turmoil within the soul for many days and many nights, but hope is forever in the Savior. God is the lover of our souls and He sent His only Son to die so that our souls could be saved and live with Him. He wants no soul to perish. The Bible says, "… but is longsuffering toward us, not willing that any should perish but that all should come to repentance" (2 Peter 3:9). The saved soul dwells in the body and is owned by our Lord and Savior Jesus Christ. Every soul has a dwelling place with or without Almighty God. All must decide where their soul will reside.

The Only Price That Could Be Paid

We live in a fallen world where sin abounds causing chaos, pain, and suffering, but it's best to *"Suffer God's Way"*. Suffering God's way may seem to be a strikingly peculiar statement because many believe God does not allow His children to suffer or that people should not suffer at all. Many questioned why God would allow suffering? We must remember that Jesus Christ suffered unconscionably for our sakes on the cross. There is only one that saves the weary, lost, or shattered soul and His name is Jesus Christ. His life was *the only price that could be paid* for the entire world's debt of sin. Everyone has the propensity to sin. Jesus Christ's death allowed sinful mankind to be acceptable in the presence of Almighty God. Many of the ways that human beings suffered, Jesus Christ also suffered, yet He did not sin. Many will suffer in this world, but the key is not to sin while suffering. Don't turn away from God because of *soul pain*, draw near to Him to receive peace. He will always be a loving Father because He is love.

Satan utilizes sin to rob and deceive all people. Satan relishes the negative effects of sin and uses *soul pain* to achieve the things he sets out to accomplish. The Bible says, "But I am afraid that just as Eve was deceived by the serpent's cunning, your minds may somehow be led astray from your sincere and pure devotion to Christ" (2 Corinthians 11:3). Satan will do anything to dominate and control the mind, heart, and soul of God's people. Satan's goal is to rob us of our loving relationship with Jesus Christ. He welcomes spiritual destruction caused by *soul pain*. While we try to find relief from *soul pain*, Satan assaults our souls for pleasure. Jesus Christ is the only power that can defeat the schemes and deceit of Satan. He is the only one that heals the weary soul. The price He paid on the cross for all the people was right. Only faith in Him gives us the right to be called children of God and be acceptable in His presence.

When we see distorted reflections in the mirror, we need peace in our souls. Distortion comes in different ways. Sin can distort the truth. Personal realities can distort the truth. *Soul pain* can distort the truth. Also, confusion in the mind can play tricks on what is seen by the eyes. Believers must walk by faith and not by sight. Satan uses the eyes to create an identity crisis that seems very real and sometimes detrimental steps are taken to correct the unwanted image.

We must remember our identity is found solely in Jesus Christ and thank God humanity is always beautiful in His eyes because we all are fearfully and wonderfully made. God graciously creates a void within in human soul that only Jesus Christ can fill. Whenever doubt arise about difficulties in life, believers can always depend on God's Word to know how to think and react to those difficulties and do what pleases God at the same time. Lovingly the believer has God the Holy Spirit to intervene with His power when the God approved response seems too hard.

Events in the world can cause stress, hardship, and disappointment that weigh heavy on the soul of man, but God the Holy Spirit gives believers spiritual instruction, guidance, and wisdom during those problematic times. Being led by God the Holy Spirit will bring conviction to the soul, and transformation to the heart, and mind. God has given His children many promises, but many of those promises are missed because believers lack the proper connection. The right connection brings us into a right relationship with God. We also inherit wonderful gifts from God's love, truth, and hope in the Lord and Savior Jesus Christ.

When we have guilty consciences associated with sin, there should be an urgency within to do things that please God. In doing so, the heart becomes responsive in knowing that God cannot look upon sin. Therefore, God cannot look upon us. Jesus Christ came down from a most holy place to gift the world with this new revelation. The Old Testament proclaimed the world needed a Savior. The New Testament proclaimed the Savior walked the earth, died, and was raised from the dead. Believers proclaim Jesus Christ; the Savior is alive and His spirit dwells within them as He sits at the right hand of Almighty God. The Bible says, "… you are to give him the name Jesus, because he will save his people from their sins" (Matthew 1:21). *Soul pain* may be present in lives of believers, but we can access continual joy as we remain connected to the right source, which is Almighty God. He is the lover of our souls. How sweet is the lover of our souls?

Conclusion

క్రిక్రిక్రిక్రిక్రి

As the author of this book, I have been transparent about events in my life, God's divine healing of my *soul pain,* and my desire to share God's truth and love as I know it. *Soul pain* does not have to be a staple in anyone's life. The only answer to end *soul pain* is Jesus Christ. Through the gospel of Jesus Christ, *soul pain* can be seen for what it is, a God hater. Jesus Christ suffered physical pain, *soul pain*, and momentary abandonment from His Father. The gospel enables believers to see Jesus Christ as our hope in the world. The gospel teaches us to be wise and shrewd when *soul pain* comes. *Soul pain* destroys, but the gospel gives life. Jesus Christ was my solace to deal with unthinkable moles- tation, emotional, verbal, and mental abuse. Faith gave me listen- ing ears to hear God when He spoke to me to live out His word in love. God's Word is the only manual of absolute truth. It is the manual believers are to live by every day. God's Word slays *soul pain* to its core.

God loves the world so much, He lowered Himself to become human. Through His Son, the world gained access to Almighty God. He shared and showered love on all. Agape love found me on that warm evening while I was watching *"The Greatest Story Ever Told."* Jesus Christ's death became very real to me that very night. Jesus Christ revealed the true God of Heaven to me. When I totally surrendered to Jesus Christ as my Lord and Savior, my life changed forever. God the Holy Spirit helped me commune and pray to God the Father daily. The Bible says, "And pray in the Spirit on all occasions with all kinds of prayers and requests. With this in mind, be alert and always keep on praying for all the Lord's people" (Ephesians 6:18). Some may see my life through my burdens and *soul pain*, but God's grace was the nonverbal strength that sustained me. My gift to Jesus Christ was to surrender my imperfect life to Him and live through His perfection. He changed me spiritually, and to this day I must be perceptive to the leading of God the Holy Spirit so that I can live righteously.

Satan came in my life at an early age to destroy the soul of a trusting child. My young soul was shattered into many pieces because of poor choices made by my parents. However, God had other plans for my life. My praying grandmother impacted my life for Jesus Christ.

Spiritual warfare struck my heart, mind, and soul anytime and anyplace. The battle was ongoing, but the Godhead was in the midst. I will always praise God for protecting me with His love and power. I praise Jesus Christ for being my protector, my redeemer, and my Savior while drinking from a bitter cup of suffering, God's miraculous grace changed my heart for good. The Bible says, "O give thanks unto the LORD; for he is good: for his mercy endureth forever" (Psalm 136:1). I took hold of the Word of God that is rooted in truth. God's agape love was my defense against the robber. The Bible says, "Therefore, submit to God. Resist the devil and he will flee from you" (James 4:7). Prayer was my choice of weapon against *soul pain* and the schemes of Satan.

Jesus Christ is my rock to hold onto when the storms of life cause me to become weary. God's mercy and love are what every person needs to survive in this world. Jesus Christ saturated me with His love, which brought me into a right relationship with the God of Heaven. Jesus Christ carried me through my dark times, and I thanked Him for everything that happens in my life good and bad. His precious blood was shed to purchase my soul from damnation and brings me into the fellowship of His Glorious Church.

My soul rejoices and my heart longs to be in communion with God every time I see God's splendor. I never blame God for the circumstances in my life or question His ability to help and heal me in troubled times because I know He is Almighty God. I know nothing is impossible for Him. God's promises assisted me in combating the many life-altering effects of *soul pain*. I tasted the living water that flowed into my soul from Jesus Christ. The Bible says, "Jesus said to her, 'Everyone who drinks of this water will be thirsty again, but whoever drinks of the water that I will give him will never be thirsty again. The water that I will give him will become in him a spring of water welling up to eternal life'" (John 4:13-14).

I am so blessed to be connected to Almighty God through God the Holy Spirit. He fought for my mental, physical, and spiritual wellbeing. I am amazed to see how God's Word is interwoven into every facet of my life. I am humbled and in awe that Almighty God would allow me to be in His Kingdom. I have joy in my heart to know that I am one of the billons of people in the world that is a child of Almighty God. As a child of God, I am not to walk as a victim, but walk in victory. I know I am not the only person in the world that has or will endure abuse by the hands of their parents or someone else. Nevertheless, the sting of *soul pain* has been removed, but the internal scars will always remain. My heart is sensitive to the many people who have experienced the rot of *soul pain*; those who do not know where to turn; and those who do not know they are experiencing pain in their soul.

Faith in Jesus Christ can take captive every memory of a traumatic act of abuse and change a broken heart into a heart that glorifies Almighty God and overflows with God's love. Seeking and serving Jesus Christ cannot be summed up with mere words, but I must acknowledge that being an ambassador of Jesus Christ is of the highest honor. It is righteous actions that bring about peace, love, and happiness in the soul. Believers must seek God's promises always – even in the dark valley of *soul pain*. Through the bitterness of *soul pain*, sweet miraculous blessings can be realized. Each believer is a single ray of light from Jesus Christ that shines in this dark world. The unbeliever will never know the beauty of the light; but the believer will always illuminate the light of Jesus Christ.

Jesus Christ is the way for believers to live in harmony with Almighty God and each other. Believers should allow circumstances in our lives be steppingstones of godly victories. We should show the world how God delivered us from our *soul pain*. The Bible says, "and call on me in the day of trouble; I will deliver you, and you will honor me" (Psalm 50:15). Deliverance is a blessing. It is an act by God to rescue us from separation and brokenness, the trials of life, and from the many vices of human nature. In all matters of deliverance, which includes separation and brokenness, our Lord and Savior Jesus Christ is the antidote. The believer must not let anyone or anything have power over them, but Jesus Christ. Refuse to carry a "victim's spirit of brokenness."

I hope this book inspires sufferers, unbelievers, or the curious to allow God the Holy Spirit to heal them from *soul pain* and become who God created them to be. God willing, the words on these pages will provoke the reader not to settle for only knowing about Jesus Christ, but to step out of their comfort zone to love, trust, and honor Him in all things. It is desired that the accompanying workbook will grow the reader's faith in Jesus Christ.

Mankind is made acceptable before Almighty God through Jesus Christ alone. His message to the world was love and obey Almighty God. Jesus Christ is the Mediator between God and man. Hopefully, if the reader is looking for relief from *soul pain*, they can find comfort in the things that Almighty God offers. The words in this book have been poured out from a victorious sufferer's heart looking to assist others trying to find relief from their *soul pain*.

Physical healing can be seen and Almighty God is praised. Having said that, when *soul pain* comes always remember, the Godhead intervenes in the lives of God's children. Miraculously healed *soul pain*, which is unseen by the eye should be appreciated as well. This type of healing lasts forever and changes us forever.

Believers must release our *soul pain* to Jesus Christ and become totally committed to and dependent upon Him. The Christian's ultimate goal is to please Almighty God and for the world to see Jesus Christ in them. Only Almighty God can heal the sin sick soul in its darkest places. There is nothing like freedom from *soul pain* – the pain only God can heal.

God Bless You

"For he satisfies the longing soul, and the hungry soul he fills with good things". — Psalm 107:9

ক্তিক্তিক্তিক্তিক্তিক্তি

Dear Loved One,

I pray that this book will transform your heart, mind, and soul and enable you to see life through eyes of faith. May the words in this book give you wisdom and understanding of soul pain. May soul pain no longer reign in your life. Turn to Jesus Christ as your solution and problem solver. Allow God the Holy Spirit to bring clarity to your mind and transform your heart. When suffering and soul pain come into your life, do not be overcome or defined by your pain. Know that the source of soul pain does not come from God. Allow God's grace to propel you to love yourself, love others, and love your enemies. Stand on and apply God's Holy Word in your daily life.

God, please touch the life of this reader and release them from any bondage because of soul pain. God give them the path to true peace, righteousness, and unquenchable joy in Jesus Christ. Thank you, Jesus Christ, for being their Friend, Savior, and Redeemer. May their life be forever set free from the clutches of soul pain.

Amen

Author's Statement

I wrote this book because of love that Jesus Christ placed in my heart. Because of Jesus Christ, my life has changed dramatically. My family and I are living recipients of God's grace. My husband's relationship with God has become anew. I see God's hands over his life every day. My children have blessed me tremendously. The Bible says, "I will pour out my Spirit on your offspring, and my blessing on your descendants" (Isaiah 44:3). I am incredibly blessed, despite of my earlier trials in life. By God's grace, I am comfortable with the person I have become. God has allowed me to live free from the burden of guilt and anger because of my past. Jesus Christ has given me peace and the ability not to hate my enemies. I can love freely and I have unspeakable joy. Going forward with my life, I am mindful to love God with all my heart, soul, and mind in my daily walk. He allows me to be a testimony for Jesus Christ for the rest of my life, our Righteous King. I am not a perfect person, but I am spiritually maturing. This is the last section of this book, but it's not the last chapter of my life. I am still being transformed into the likeness of my Lord and Savior, Jesus Christ.

SCRIPTURE INDEX (NIV)

Introduction
1. 1 John 3:8

Prologue
1. Psalm 147:3
2. Psalm 139: 2-4
3. Hebrews 4:16

PART ONE
Chapter 1:
Silent Sufferer
1. Chapter Scripture: Psalm 27:10
2. Luke 23:34
3. Psalm 34:18
4. Jeremiah 17:9
5. Exodus 14:14
6. Romans 8:28

Chapter 2:
A Look In the Mirror
1. Chapter Scripture: Psalm 139:14
2. Matthew 6:22
3. 2 Chronicles 20:15
4. John 10:10
5. Ephesians 6:12
6. Psalm 146:8
7. Genesis 1:27

Chapter 3:
The Turmoil That Rage Within
1. Chapter Scripture: 1 Corinthian 10:13
2. Matthew 10:28
3. Genesis 6:5
4. Job 30:27
5. 1 John 3:8
6. 2 Thessalonians 2:16
7. 1 Peter 5:7

8. Proverbs 29:25
9. Proverbs 3:6

Chapter 4:
The Mind of Jesus Christ

1. Chapter Scripture: Philippians 2:5
2. 2 Timothy 1:7
3. Colossians 3:2
4. Jeremiah 33:3
5. Romans 12:2
6. 2 Corinthians 10:5
7. Philippians 4:13
8. 1 Peter 5:10
9. Ezekiel 11:5

Chapter 5:
The Godhead

1. Chapter Scripture: Colossians 2:10
2. 1 Samuel 2:2
3. Colossians 1:15
4. John 14:16
5. John 15:26
6. 1 John 4:10
7. 2 Corinthian 5:17
8. Galatians 2:20
9. Ephesians 3:17
10. John 16:13

Chapter 6:
Peace that Transcends Understanding

1. Chapter Scripture: John 14:17
2. Philippians 4:7
3. Isaiah 65:24
4. 2 Thessalonian 3:16
5. 2 Corinthians 1:3-4
6. James 1:2-4

Chapter 7:
The Act of Forgiveness

1. Chapter Scripture: Ephesians 4:32
2. John 3:16

3. Exodus 32:1
4. 1 John 2:2
5. Ephesians 4:32
6. Matthew 18:21-22
7. Ephesians 1:7
8. Matthew 19:19
9. Matthew 6:15
10. John 15:12
11. Matthew 16:4

Chapter 8:
Strength In God's Grace

1. Chapter Scripture: 2 Peter 1:2
2. Romans 3: 23-24
3. Deuteronomy 14:2
4. Deuteronomy 30:19
5. Ephesians 2:8-10
6. Romans 4:16
7. Colossians 3:17
8. 2 Timothy 2:1

Chapter 9:
Sweetness of Mercy

1. Chapter Scripture: Luke 6:36
2. Psalm 103:8
3. Romans 9:15
4. Psalm 145:9
5. Genesis 3:21
6. Genesis 21:1
7. Exodus 32:9-14
8. John 3:17
9. Matthew 5:7
10. Psalm 103:17
11. Romans 12:2
12. Hebrews 4:16
13. Exodus 20:12
14. 2 Corinthians 9:8
15. Luke 17:3-4

Chapter 10:
A Servant's Heart

1. Chapter Scripture: Ezekiel 36:26
2. Mark 10:45
3. Mark 12:31
4. 1 Corinthians 13:4-7
5. Colossians 3:23
6. Matthew 10:42
7. Ephesians 2:10

A Willing Vessel

1. 2 Timothy 2:21
2. Matthew 6:13
3. Psalm 4:3

PART TWO
Chapter 11:
Life Can Be Bittersweet and Sweet

1. Chapter 12: John 10:10
2. Psalm 34:13
3. 1 Peter 1:2
4. Hebrews 11:1

Chapter 12:
All About Me

1. Chapter 12: 2 Corinthians 5:17
2. Revelations 2:4
3. Psalm 103:2
4. James 1:2-3

Chapter 13:
Return to My First Love

1. Chapter 12: 2 Corinthians 5:15
2. 2 Corinthians 6:14
3. Psalm 34:14
4. Malachi 2:16
5. 1 Corinthian 7:13-14
6. Ezekiel 36:26
7. Psalm 147:4

    4. John 14:1

    5. John 14:27

    6. Romans 5:5

Chapter 18:
God's Transforming Love and A Transformed Life

    1. Chapter Scripture: 1 John 4:10

    2. Jerimiah 24:7

    3. John 1:12

    4. 2 Corinthians 5:17

    5. Psalm 34:17-18

    6. 2 Corinthians 12:9

    7. Genesis 50:20

    8. 1 John 4:16

    9. Romans 10:9

    10. 2 Thessalonians 3:3

    11. Romans 12:29

    12. Ephesians 2:10

    13. 2 Corinthians 3:18

Much More to Come

    1. Romans 12:2

    2. Proverbs 3:1-2, 8

Part ThreeThe Most High Dwelling Place

    1. Psalm 91:1, 9,10

    2. Joshua 1:9

Chapter 19:
Suffer God's Way

    1. Chapter Scripture: 1 Peter 4:19

    2. Romans 8:7

    3. Psalm 94:11

    4. 1 John 3:4

    5. Romans 5:5

    6. 1 Corinthian 1:10

    7. Isaiah 41:10

    8. 2 Corinthian 7:10

    9. James 1:17

10. 1 Peter 2:9
11. 1 Peter 5:10

Chapter 20:
The Distorted Reflection

1. Chapter Scripture: 2 Corinthians 4:8-10
2. 1 Corinthians 6:19-20
3. James 1:23-24
4. Proverbs 30:5
5. Ephesians 4:18-19
6. Jeremiah 1:5
7. 2 Corinthians 5:7
8. Psalm 139:13
9. Colossians 1:12-14
10. Psalm 30:5
11. Philippians 1:20
12. Psalm 27:14

Chapter 21:
Sin Abound

1. Chapter Scripture: James 4:17
2. Genesis 3:17
3. Romans 3:23
4. Habakkuk 1:13
5. John 18:37
6. Genesis 6:5
7. John 8:34
8. Isaiah 64:6
9. 1 John 2:16
10. Luke 4:18
11. Psalm 11:5
12. 1 Timothy 2:9
13. Romans 7:15
14. 1 John 3:4
15. Isaiah 59:2
16. Psalm 5:4
17. 1 John 1:8
18. 1 Peter 2:24
19. Isaiah 1:18
20. Romans 5:9

21. Psalm 62:8
22. Deuteronomy 4:29:31
23. Proverbs 16:5
24. Proverbs 16:18
25. 1 John 1:9
26. Titus 3:4-6
27. Romans 8:18

Chapter 22:
Robbery

1. Chapter Scripture: John 10:10
2. 1 Peter 5:8
3. 1 Corinthians 6:19
4. Romans 7:5
5. John 8:44
6. 2 Corinthians 11:3
7. John 20:27
8. Isaiah 14:14
9. Matthew 7:15
10. Psalm 62:10
11. Ephesians 6:11
12. Revelations 20:2

Chapter 23:
Is There No Relief For My Pain

1. Chapter Scripture: John 16:33
2. Romans 8:35
3. Job 2:7
4. Job 1:22
5. Psalm 55:22
6. Revelations 21:4
7. Psalm 56:8
8. Psalm 73:26
9. Psalm 119:71
10. 1 Thessalonians 5:18

Chapter 24:
Separation and Brokenness

1. Chapter Scripture: Psalm 34:18
2. Romans 3:10

3. Isaiah 53:6
4. Proverbs 18:1
5. Genesis 4:7
6. Matthew 27:46
7. Philippians 2:8
8. Jerimiah 17:9
9. Isaiah 59:2
10. 1Timothy 6:34
11. John 3:3
12. Genesis 19:26
13. Revelations 21:4
14. Acts 2:38
15. Romans 8:38-39
16. 2 Corinthian 5:17
17. 2 Corinthians 10:3-5

Chapter 25:
God the Holy Spirit – Power to Live By

1. Chapter Scripture: Galatians 5:22-23
2. 2 Peter 2:21
3. Romans 6:12
4. Isaiah 55:8
5. Mark 7:13
6. John 15:5
7. 2 Corinthians 4:16
8. Romans 8:11
9. Luke 24:49
10. 1 John 4:16
11. Genesis 1:2
12. 1 Corinthians 2:10a
13. 1 Corinthians 2:10b
14. Romans 8:27
15. John 14:26
16. Romans 8:26
17. Romans 8:14
18. Ephesians 4:30
19. 1 Corinthians 12:11
20. 1 Corinthians 6:19
21. Acts 1:8
22. Ephesians 6:12

Chapter 26:
Spiritual Peace

1. Chapter Scripture: 2 Thessalonians 3:16
2. Proverbs 12:25
3. Isaiah 48:22
4. 1 Thessalonians 5:17
5. Numbers 6:26
6. Hebrews 13:8

Chapter 27:
Transformation of the Heart

1. Chapter Scripture: Proverbs 4:23
2. Matthew 15:18-19
3. Jeremiah 15:18
4. 1 Peter 14:12
5. John 13:34
6. Psalm 32:11
7. Psalm 51:10
8. Titus 2:11
9. Ephesians 4:32
10. Ezekiel 36:26
11. Proverbs 4:23

Chapter 28:
Transformation of the Mind

1. Chapter Scripture: Romans 12:2
2. 2 Corinthians 10:5
3. 1 Corinthians 2:11
4. Psalm 94:11
5. 2 Timothy 2:7

Chapter 29:
Rebuke the Victim Spirit

1. Chapter Scripture: James 1:2-3
2. Galatians 5:19-21
3. Romans 8:7
4. John 10:10
5. 1 John 4:1
6. 2 Corinthians 5:17
7. John 6:63

8. Psalm 50:15
9. Job 42:10

Chapter 30:
Connected to the Right Source

1. Chapter Scripture: Romans 8:38-39
2. Genesis 3:23
3. Jeremiah 15:18
4. John 1:12
5. Romans 8:26
6. Hebrew 10:19
7. Hebrews 13:8
8. John 15:26
9. 1 Corinthians 2:9-10
10. Romans 5:3-5

Chapter 31:
The Void Only God Can Fill

1. Chapter Scripture: Psalms 37:4-5
2. Haggai 1:6
3. Matthew 5:6
4. James 1:14-15
5. 1 Peter 2:11
6. Romans 12:2
7. 2 Corinthians 5:17
8. Ephesians 4:22-24
9. Psalm 42:2
10. Galatians 5:13
11. Romans 6:11

Chapter 32:
Jesus Christ the Mediator, He Is the Way

1. Chapter Scripture: John 14:6
2. Proverbs 16:4
3. Psalm 32:7
4. 1 Timothy 2:5
5. John 1:14
6. 2 Thessalonians 1:12
7. Psalm 4:3
8. Ephesians 1:22-23

9. Exodus 15:2
10. Mark 4:22
11. Colossians 1:16
12. Romans 8:9
13. Exodus 14:14
14. 2 Samuel 22:3-4
15. Genesis 3:15

Chapter 33:
The Word of God "Brings Forth Life Not Heartache"

1. Chapter Scripture: Psalm 119:105
2. Psalm 119:160
3. 1 Timothy 6:3-4
4. 2 Timothy 3:12
5. 1 Samuel 12:15
6. John 1: 1-4
7. Proverbs 30:5
8. Luke 8:11
9. Matthew 7:24
10. John17:17

Chapter 34:
Lover of Our Souls

1. Chapter Scripture: Ezekiel 18:4
2. Mark 10:18
3. Isaiah 53:6
4. Mark 8:36
5. John 6:64
6. Mark 16:16
7. Isaiah 59:2
8. Matthew 11:29
9. Jeremiah 31:25
10. 1 John 2:15
11. Psalm 103:1-5
12. Psalm 23: 3
13. Genesis 2:7
14. 1 John 4:7
15. Job 33:4
16. 2 Peter 3:9

The Only Price That Could Be Paid

1. 2 Corinthians 11:3
2. Matthew 1:21

Conclusion

1. Ephesians 6:18
2. Psalm 136:1
3. James 4:17
4. John 4:13-14
5. Psalm 50:15

God Bless You

Psalm 107:9

Author's Statement

Isaiah 44:3

References

1. Lewis, C.S. ed., 2001. In: *The Screwtape Letters*. New York, NY: HarperCollins Publications, p.5.

2. Lucado, Max. "A Heart Like His" Chapter 1. In *Just Like Jesus,* 8-9. Nashville, TN, Word Publishing, 1998

3. Yonat Shimron. Most American believe, but not always in the God of the Bible, *Religion News Service,* April 23, 2018

https://religionnews.com/2018/04/25/most-americans-believe-but-not-always-in-the-god-of-the-bible/

4. Wisdom's Corner: A Lamp to My Feet, *Apologetic Press,* March 14, 2018

   https://www.apologeticspress.org/apPubPage.aspx?-pub=2&issue=776&article=2307

Goodreads.com. 2020. A Quote by George Macdonald. https://www.goodreads.com/quotes/8131121-never-tell-a-child-you-have-a-soul-teach-him

5. The Holy Bible: New International Standard Version

6. The Holy Bible: King James Version

7. The Holy Bible: New King James Version

8. The Holy Bible: English Standard Version

Book Purchase

Freedom From Soul Pain - Seeing the Presence of God Though Pain

ERHURTTAUTHOR.COM
Women Seeking the Kingdom.com

Contact the Author

ERHURTTAUTHOR.COM
PO Box 426
Owings Mills, Maryland 21117

Website: ERHURTTAUTHOR.COM

Email: Contact@ERHURTTAUTHOR.COM

www.ingramcontent.com/pod-product-compliance
Lightning Source LLC
Chambersburg PA
CBHW060906120626
46553CB00001B/231